THE O.S.S. AND I

THE O.S.S. AND I

By WILLIAM J. MORGAN

W · W · NORTON & COMPANY · INC · *New York*

COPYRIGHT © 1957 BY WILLIAM J. MORGAN

LIBRARY OF CONGRESS CATALOG CARD NO. 57-5988

AN UNCOMMON VALOR REPRINT EDITION
Complete and Unabridged
Printed in the United States of America

ISBN: 978-1951682866

To TONI

Contents

1. Don't Tell a Soul — 11
2. Pemberley — 22
3. Train Test — 31
4. Obstacles, Minefields, and Acid Baths — 35
5. Groupstacle — 45
6. The Pond — 52
7. The Barbed-Wire Barrier — 57
8. The Criminal-Gang Problem — 60
9. Chief and Recruit — 70
10. You're the Boss — 77
11. Red Is Blue and Up Is Down — 86
12. Elbows on the Table — 94
13. Taping the Candidates — 105
14. The Road to the Isles — 110
15. Getting Closer — 126

16.	The Monastery	133
17.	Hook-up	148
18.	Action Station	163
19.	"Hands Up!"	170
20.	"Cheecago Gangstair"	183
21.	How to Blow a Bridge	192
22.	Get in Place	203
23.	Ambush at Pont de la Fargo	212
24.	"We'll Shoot Them Ourselves"	227
25.	Camp Life	241
26.	Lagic	250
27.	"Lift Up Their Skirts"	260
28.	A Communist and a Viscount	270
29.	Secret Mission	277

PHOTOGRAPHS

Between pages 142 and 143

THE O.S.S. AND I

1 · Don't Tell a Soul

IT WAS the hottest day in the torrid summer of 1943, made worse by the famous humidity of Washington, D.C. We officer candidates at the AGO School were sticking to our chairs as we listened to an army captain, formerly a Kentucky judge, giving a lecture on courts-martial regulations. I was summoned out of the room, ushered into a small, stuffy interview room and faced by two strangers, one in civilian clothes and the other an army captain with the shield insignia of the Adjutant-General on his collar. They introduced themselves, asked me to sit down, and then said, "We have looked over the records of all students in this present OCS class and we have come to the conclusion that you have the kind of background we are interested in."

Well, that was pleasant news to my ears. You don't often get compliments in the army.

They asked, "Are you willing to undertake hazardous duties?" "Are you willing to go overseas?" "Are you willing to parachute from a plane behind enemy lines, if necessary?" "Are you willing to go in by submarine and be landed alone on an enemy coast?"

I was puzzled by these questions but I truthfully answered, "Yes."

They were pleased with my answers, shook my hand warmly, and gave me a long, detailed, involved personal biographic form to fill out and mail to Que Building in Washington. "Try to get this in to us in a few days," said the captain. "And don't tell anybody about this—not a soul," cautioned the civilian.

I couldn't quite figure out this secrecy. Ever since I got my Ph.D. at Yale, I had been a professional psychologist. The army was always harping on putting the right man in the right job. Though it wasn't what I wanted, I expected to be put behind a desk to deal with problems of personnel selection and classification. What was secret or confidential about that?

"May I ask what department of the army you represent?" I inquired. "Yes," answered the captain, "but don't talk about it. O.S.S."

"Well," I said to myself, "it begins to make sense." I remembered hearing one of the instructors in the School talk about O.S.S.—the Office of Scientific Services, he said—where they were conducting important research work on guided missiles, submarine detection devices, and whatnot. I must be going to do personnel work there.

During the next few days I completed the Personal History statement, all three copies of it, and sent them in. Soon I received orders to report to General William Donovan, Commanding O.S.S., Que Building. I wired General

Donovan in advance and gave him my ETA (estimated time of arrival). I had read in one of the books in the AG School that that was the proper thing to do, and I fully expected Donovan to be there and greet me when I reported for duty on Labor Day in September 1943—a brand new second lieutenant.

I had my first shock when I reached Que Building and found it was the headquarters not of the Office of *Scientific* Services but of the Office of *Strategic* Services, whatever that was. The guard at the door had never heard of me. He sent me to a receptionist, who asked me to fill out a slip of paper with my name, address, phone number. I was then sent upstairs to the Personnel Sergeant, and registered for duty in O.S.S.

For the next week or so I was shunted from office to office. Time and again they asked the same questions. The answers were all in the Personal History Statement which had cost me so much labor to fill out. I began to feel like the six-year-old boy who was asked by the psychologist, "Are you a boy or a girl?" "Girl," he replied. When his father remonstrated, he said, "If that man doesn't know the answer, why should I tell him?"

While wandering down the corridors of Que Building one day I spotted the clean-cut, handsome captain who had interviewed me at Fort Washington. He was sitting behind a desk surrounded by a crowd of people. I bounced in, stretched my hand across his desk, and said, "Captain Clean-Cut, how do you do? Remember me?"

He shook my hand, mainly because it was in his way. "No, I don't remember you," he said.

"Oh, you must remember me," I implored. "You and Mr. Civilian Clothes interviewed me at Fort Washington only about a month ago."

At this the handsome captain jumped out of his chair, raced around his desk, grabbed me by the arm, and dragged me to a far corner of the room. "You must never, never mention that man's name again, never," he whispered into my ear. Feeling like a naughty boy, I went back into the corridor.

One day I found my way to the library and asked for the newspaper and periodical files on O.S.S. The librarian delivered them to me in batches. She was clearly delighted that someone was willing to read the clippings about O.S.S. and General Donovan from the *New York Times*, the *Washington Post, Time Magazine, Collier's* and the *Chicago Tribune*, which she had so carefully collected and pasted into scrapbooks.

I had been desperately trying to find out what O.S.S. was all about. Nobody would tell me. The O.S.S. security system was almost perfect. The guards, receptionists, sergeants, officers, interviewers had all been thoroughly and completely indoctrinated on security precautions. But here it was, all the dope I could ask for. "Roosevelt sends Wild Bill on Secret Missions . . . Colonel Donovan, the Man Nobody Knows . . . Our Espionage System Abroad . . . C.O.I. Becomes O.S.S. . . . No More Pearl Harbors . . . O.S.S.: The Eyes and Ears of the United States." News reporters, editorial writers, columnists—all of them briefed me on O.S.S.

It was all perfectly plain. O.S.S. was the United States

intelligence agency engaged in espionage, counter-espionage, sabotage, subversion, black psychological warfare, and guerrilla operations. O.S.S. covered the globe. Its agents were everywhere. They listened to Hitler's rantings; they whispered into Hirohito's ear; they decoyed the enemy generals into making false moves; mingling with the common hordes they spread slanderous rumors to bring about political revolutions; in the armaments factories of the enemy they tossed the right parts into the wrong bins, or tossed the right parts into the right bins but without cotter pins holding the parts of the parts together. What an outfit!

As a youngster I had dreamed of travel and adventure —Revolutionaries hiding behind trees and rocks and shooting at British Redcoats, Daniel Boone crawling on his belly through the brush and taking a deadly bead on an Indian Savage—but with 20/200 vision in one eye I had no chance of getting into West Point. Now, after years of desk work as a psychologist, I could maybe play a fighting role in this war. But I had to play my cards right. One false move and I would find myself right behind a desk again, giving psychological tests.

My chance came within a few days. I was invited to talk once more with a lieutenant-colonel who had a huge office up on the hill, overlooking The Brewery. Before the war he had been the foremost expert on shirts in the country. The carpet can't have been more than three inches thick, but I had the feeling of sinking into it up to my knees as I walked across the auditorium-sized room to the far corner where the lieutenant-colonel had his desk. He asked me to sit in the best and biggest of his many leather chairs. Then he offered me a cigarette and lighted it for me. "I would like to continue the discussions we had the other day," he began. "I'm sorry we can't find your records. But I'm sure we will be able to straighten out the matter. *Do you have any idea what O.S.S. might have hired you for?*"

This was it, my big chance. I fidgeted a little in my chair. Slowly and carefully I turned my head over my left shoulder. The door was open but it was far away. Nobody else was in the room. Just as slowly and carefully I turned my head over my right shoulder and surveyed the room with my right eye—the one with the 20/200 vision. So what if I could see only a big blur of a shadow? You must be discreet. All the best spy books tell you so. Then I put the cigarette to my lips and let out a faint puff of smoke. I searched for his eyes and looked right at him.

I said softly, "Maybe it's because I speak French and German fluently."

"*Of course, of course!*" he exclaimed. "Which do you prefer?"

"France," I replied.

O.S.S. had hired a Harvard Professor whose chief duty was to test persons for fluency in French. I had had only three years of French and I was not at all sure I would pass. He made an appointment to test me but the next day he phoned me to cancel the appointment and schedule another one. That gave me an idea. I cancelled the next appointment. So we went along, cancelling each other's appointments or finding ourselves unable to agree on the time for the next one. I never had to take the test, and I never permitted myself to be drawn into telephone conversation in French.

The next hurdle was the physical exam. To get overseas I had to have a medical clearance for combat duty. Clearance, clearance, clearance. The army is full of them, and so was O.S.S. I was sent to the medical unit at the Pentagon, and, as usual, everything was fine until the doctor came to my right eye. "Read the last line on the chart," he said as he covered my left eye.

"I think I can read the first line," I said, "it seems to be the letter E. But it's fuzzy and I can't tell which way it's facing."

Within a few minutes he handed me the report of the physical exam. Stamped across it diagonally, in big, bold, red letters, was "NOT FIT FOR OVERSEAS OR COMBAT DUTY."

This dashed my hopes. What could I do? If I turned it in to the O.S.S. medical officer, as I had been instructed, he would stop the cutting of my overseas orders. I kept the report for one day, two days, three days—and looked at it many, many times. On the fourth day my orders were issued. I was to leave for Europe in thirty-six hours. If I turned in the report, the orders would be cancelled. I held on to the report. On the last day I went about getting the financial, legal and other clearances. I postponed going to the medical office until late in the afternoon. It was on the second floor of the garage, across from Heurich's Brewery. At the foot of the stairs I took one last look at the medicophysical report. Suddenly I knew what to do. I tore it up into small pieces and threw it to the wind. Then I walked upstairs to see the medical officer, and waited my turn in line.

When he came to me he said, "Morgan, you should have reported here right after the exam at the Pentagon."

"Sorry, Doc, you know the way it is just before you go."

"Let me have the report of the exam you took at the Pentagon."

"Oh, yes," and I began fumbling through my pockets —the blouse, the shirt, the trousers, all twelve pockets. Couldn't find it. I searched in some pockets two or three times, and turned them inside out. "I know I had it," I said, as I began a systematic search of all my pockets again. There were many others waiting behind me in line. The medical officer grew impatient.

"Well, can you remember what it said?" he asked.

"Oh, it had some words stamped on it, overseas or combat duty, or something like that."

"Okay, okay," he said hurriedly. "Sign here."

I did. The next man stepped forward and I went back to my room to pack my gear for the trip.

My gear consisted of everything but an automatic dishwasher. I had a .32 and a .45 pistol; a .22 pistol with a silencer; an ordinary blackjack; a spring-snapper cosh blackjack; a camera and plenty of film; two sleeping-bags, one from Abercrombie and Fitch; a heavy box full of time-pencils and other detonating and explosive devices; a regular army knife; a special "Fairbairn" killer stiletto; and fishskins. When I asked the Supply Sergeant to what use the fishskins could be put he said they were excellent as grenade covers, and that men going to Moscow would order them by the gross.

Within a few days we were on the high seas in a ten-thousand-ton vessel which before the war had plied across the Caribbean in the banana trade. The trip was not very exciting, even though one day the escorting destroyers ash-canned a German submarine which had sent torpedoes in our direction. I managed to win fifteen dollars at poker.

We landed in Scotland and made our way to Edinburgh, where we would take the train to London. At the Edinburgh railroad station, the Colonel in charge broke us up into three squads. One squad was to get our baggage into the Station, one was to scrounge for food, and the third, which included me as well as the Colonel himself, boarded the London Express to see what spare space we could latch onto. The train began to move, and before we could jump out we were speeding on our way to London. Early next morning we arrived at King's Cross Station. Later that morning the rest of our group arrived, and later still, the baggage. But it was not ours. It was parachutes and gear belonging to some fighter pilots from Texas who had been with us on the banana boat. I hope my hardware, which I had so carefully garnered in Washington, was of some use to the Texan flyers. I never saw it again.

When I reported to O.S.S. Headquarters in Grosvenor Street, a major gave me the sad news. My personnel records had been found in Washington. I was to be flown back to the States for duty as a classification psychologist at Washington Headquarters.

In desperation I said, "A psychologist is a pretty useful guy to have around. Don't you need any here?"

"That all depends, Lieutenant. Are you willing to work with the British?"

"What's the deal, Major?" I inquired.

It was this. O.S.S. and the British Intelligence Services were working hand in glove. The Britishers, old and wise in the intelligence game, were training Americans in the British intelligence schools in England and Scotland. But they had been disappointed in the calibre and qualifications of American agents and operatives. (Agents and operatives are polite words for spies.) The British now insisted that all intelligence candidates, including Americans, must pass the British Selection Assessment Board (SAB) at Pemberley, before being accepted for further training. SAB was rejecting two out of three American candidates, even after they had been selected, trained, and briefed in the States. The standards of SAB were high and, moreover, American attitudes and behavior were often misunderstood by the British.

Would I be interested in going to Pemberley as the American representative on SAB to help them in their work and to interpret American behavior patterns?

"*Of course,*" I exclaimed. "And when that job is done could I be given the opportunity of going behind the lines as an operative myself?"

"Good. I'm sure that can be arranged. You pick 'em now

and spy later," he said. I'm sure he never gave his promise another thought.

A few days later, after an hour's journey by train and lorry, I found myself at the gates of a secluded country estate called Pemberley. It belonged to a titled Englishman but the War Office had taken it over. Tea was being served in the Officers' Mess. I was pleasantly surprised at the warmth of my welcome. I was met with smiles and handshakes and they seemed genuinely glad to have me with them. An American, especially a psychologist, was still an oddity in England, and they were curious to find out what he had to say and how he would behave. I was also useful as a living reference library on customs, conditions, and traditions in the States. Later I learned that each of my hosts had been especially picked for this Staff on the basis of his outstanding work in espionage or counter-espionage. I was the only tyro in the bunch. And yet these men made me feel they had so much to learn from me!

2 · Pemberley

ONE OF the psychologists in Hitler's Wehrmacht was a remarkable man named Simoneit. He took to heart the principle that there is a world of difference between what a man says he will do and what he actually does. In selecting officer candidates Simoneit would watch each candidate marching in formation and shouting orders to a platoon, listen to his talk in class and at table, and find out what was said of him by his fellow candidates and his superiors, by his friends and his enemies. Simoneit recorded all these observations and analyzed them in terms of the jobs for which the man was being considered. If the evidence from observing a candidate in a natural situation was inconclusive, Simoneit would arrange situations as nearly as possible like those met in actual warfare, and see how the man behaved. As far as they could, he and his associates worked unobtrusively and unknown. The terrible effectiveness of the Nazi war machine owed much to the cold and calculating way in which Simoneit picked the officers who led the Germans into battle.

When war broke out, the British were obliged to select

large numbers of officers in a hurry. In doing so they developed a system which combined the best features of German psychology, and in particular the techniques of Simoneit, with the scientific, psychometric approach of American psychology. This system has come to be known as "assessment."

On my first evening at Pemberley the new group of spy candidates was assembled to hear a talk by the Commanding Officer, Colonel Carey, a solid bulldog of a man. He had a trick of twirling the ends of his bushy grey eyebrows while he talked, just as some men twirl the tips of their mustaches. "You will be here for four days," he said. "You will be tested by psychologists, interrogated by psychiatrists, called on to solve all sorts of individual and group problems under the whiplash of the Military Testing Officers, and then finally interviewed by me. This is what we call assessment. Do your best, because your future in intelligence will depend upon your showing here."

I was invited to join one of the groups of candidates and go through the assessment with them so as to get their point of view. There was another American in my group, who soon made himself disliked by his team-mates and by anyone else who would listen to him. He claimed to have made one hundred and sixty-three parachute jumps as a barnstorming daredevil, to have been a deep-sea diver, an airline pilot, and an automobile speed-racer; to speak French, Spanish, and German; and to have starred in Hollywood motion pictures. The others would shout him down and demand proof, but he always contrived to produce it—newspaper clippings, snapshots, testimonials, idiomatic backchat in the three languages. At the end of his stay at Pemberley he was failed as a team-worker but given an exceptionally high rating as a lone wolf operative, with the reservation that his success would depend on how far he could cut down his boasting. He went into France several months before the Normandy invasion and, posing as a German, joined a German army unit. When the fighting became fierce he made his way to the American line with vital order-of-battle information. His coolness, self-assurance, and talent for plausible lying won him the Distinguished Service Cross.

At the end of their four-day assessment, candidates were given a rating. The Rating Scale was: A, outstanding; B, above average; C, average; D, poor; E, failure. The rating was always in reference to a specific assignment. If a candidate was being considered for one of two assignments, he was given two ratings—for instance, instructor, B; radio operator, D.

After I had been through the assessment grind myself I was asked whether I would prefer to work at Pemberley as a psychologist pure and simple or as a Military Testing Officer (MTO). For a number of reasons I chose to be an MTO. I wanted to become well acquainted with the other MTO's, all of whom had been in the field and could give me pointers. Besides, the MTO's worked mostly out of doors, and I was anxious to keep in shape, ready to go into France whenever the chance came. For another thing, as an MTO I would have much more opportunity to talk with the French candidates, brush up my French on them during the problems and at lunch, and pick up what I could about the attitudes of the French people. I must learn as much as possible about France and French if I were to gamble on staying alive there as a spy.

The MTO who taught me most was Jack. Before the war Jack had worked at the Crédit Lyonnais in Paris, and under this cover had been a spy for the British. Small, blond, and debonair, he spoke French with no trace of accent and could pass anywhere as a Frenchman. When I met him he had just finished organizing his second espionage net. He would parachute into France and go about his business and in a few weeks' time a submarine would pick him up at a rendezvous on the coast. He had had several narrow escapes. Once he had had to flee across the Pyrenees and was jailed for two weeks by the Spanish Government. On another mission he took with him a young Lieutenant just out of Sandhurst and full of poise and snap. Jack kept telling him, "Forget you're a soldier. You're a French civilian now." One day they were walking down a Paris street when they met two Nazi sergeants. The Nazis came up with a Heil Hitler salute, and as their arms were rising the Lieutenant briskly acknowledged it with a British salute. Jack held his breath at this blunder —a French civilian saluting German enlisted men with the British salute! The sergeants had been saluting two officers behind the Englishmen. The Lieutenant realised at once what he had done, and there was nothing they could do except go on walking, expecting every moment to hear a shout and be seized. But no one had noticed. Next day Jack arranged to have the Lieutenant shipped back to England.

Jack told me this story to illustrate how difficult it is to work out a fool-proof cover story. Too many cover stories are developed only at the level of verbal memory, so that in moments of action the spy is betrayed by the muscle habits of his past. A cover story must be rehearsed over and over, in many different situations, in order to wipe out inconsistencies of attitude, gesture, and expression.

Candidates came to Pemberley in groups of six escorted by a Conducting Officer who spoke their own language. The Conducting Officer was a key figure. He had almost always been in the field, and he had always gone through the British espionage, sabotage, and parachute schools. He nursed the moods of the candidates, helped them to think of things to say in letters to inquisitive relatives, arranged for their transportation, reserved their hotel rooms and sometimes their entertainment, and saw to it that they prepared for their field assignments and kept out of trouble. He was with the group from the moment they gathered at the train for Pemberley, remained with them through all the training schools, and often stayed to kiss each man goodbye and shake his sweating hand when he boarded plane or submarine for enemy territory.

The Conducting Officer was a pappy to the candidates but he was also a de facto adviser to the Pemberley Staff. Living with the candidates he came to know them intimately and would tell us, "Peter is a leader. . . . Jacques can take it. . . . Keep your eye on Henri, he has queasy gumption. . . . Val has energy, but he's easily upset." These bits of advice were a great help, but we often had to make allowance for the Conducting Officer's own bias.

One of them, sensitive about his lack of education, was prone to regard products of British public schools as prudes and stuffed shirts, but he was tops in sizing up French peasants. Another, once he found a candidate to be courageous and rugged, would gloss over traits like dishonesty or sexual perversion.

All the enlisted men on the permanent staff at Pemberley—waiters, cooks, batmen, orderlies, guards—were disabled veterans of the Battle of France who were unfit for further service in the field. So also were many of the Conducting Officers, among them Achille, an amiable, stocky Belgian with a wooden leg. When he had parachuted into Belgium by moonlight the wind was gusty and he could not slow the speed or swing of his chute. As he hit the ground, his right leg cracked. The chute, puffed by the wind, dragged him along the ground. At last he freed himself from the harness, dug a hole and buried his chute and other incriminating gear, and crawled on his belly to a farmhouse. The farmer took him to a hospital which was, of course, under Nazi rule. Some of the doctors were German and I don't know just what story he told them, but they never discovered that he was a spy. The nurses were all Belgian. Achille was in a bad way and his leg had to be amputated. To a lesser man this would have been a hopeless catastrophe, but Achille, quick-witted and versatile like all good spies, altered his tactics to meet the situation. While he was confined to the hospital he managed to carry out his mission of organizing resistance in the area, by using nurses as intermediaries right under the noses of the Germans. His convalescence complete, his mission accomplished, he returned to England and went to work at once as a Conducting Officer.

Women candidates came to Pemberley under the supervision of female Conducting Officers who were usually middle-aged, married, and regarded as mature and sensible. One was a wealthy, titled woman in her late forties whose husband, a brigadier, was a prisoner of war in Germany. She was full of vigor and jollity, anxious to go behind the lines, and seized every chance of doing hazardous things to prove she was fit for the field. Whenever the women she escorted went to the parachute school she jumped with them. She had twenty-nine jumps to her credit. She had a habit of slapping me on the behind with her ping-pong paddle when we were partners in ping-pong. Another Conducting Officer was a pale, intellectual widow, whose father and husband had both been officers in the British Intelligence Service. Her father had been shot by the Nazis; her husband was "missing, presumed killed." She spoke calmly of them, as if she realised that this was the way of life her family had chosen and its occupational misfortunes, though tragic, were not unexpected.

Then there was the handsome redhead who insisted on going through the obstacle course with her group of candidates and broke her ankle. And there was a mother of five who was proud of having made thirty-eight jumps, one for each year of her life. She loved to parachute and talked about it in the matter-of-fact tone in which another woman could discuss golf or bridge.

Some of the women candidates were assessed for espionage work, usually as couriers or cut-outs. (A cut-out carries information between the principal agent in a spy chain and one of his subordinates. This helps to prevent the enemy from connecting the members of the chain with one another.) Contrary to popular belief, many of the women spies were neither young nor beautiful.

Most of the women, however, were assessed as radio operators. A former Commanding Officer at Pemberley had reasoned that men behind enemy lines were likely to seek feminine society and get themselves into trouble, and that it was better to send in, along with each resistance organizer, a woman radio operator who would also serve as his social companion. This Commanding Officer went to great lengths to match up the two personalities. It was a good idea, but he was reprimanded and transferred. The British are like that. They really approved the idea but thought it bad form to talk about it. The policy was discontinued—officially, that is.

Apart from the question of sex, the standards, for a radio operator working behind the lines are well defined. He (or she) must be intelligent, persistent, and have the mechanical skill to repair as well as operate the radio. Moreover he must enjoy working alone, and he must not be exasperated by the monotony of the job. There are such people, and psychologists use the catch-all term "introverts" to describe them. But these introverts must not be neurotic. They must be emotionally stable as well as resourceful and willing to follow orders.

I knew one girl who should never have been passed as a radio operator. Biddy, a tall, blue-eyed blonde with a ravishing figure, was dropped into France with her Commanding Officer, a Major, two months before the Normandy invasion. He was forty-five; she was twenty-one. He was humorless, efficient, and exacting; she adored dancing, nylons, and plenty of boy friends. She had no interest at all in mechanical things, and was so bored by the routine of coding and decoding that it had to be handed over to a French assistant.

For the first two months she got along fairly well with the Major. The Germans knew they had arrived and were trying to pick them up, and she had to depend on him for safety. Soon after the invasion some younger officers came over to join the team. Biddy promptly deserted her Commanding Officer and, without telling him, moved herself and her radio to another town near her new friends. This disrupted communications with London. The Major managed to find her and they had a bang-up row. He slapped her. She screamed at him. Finally they kissed and made up. After that he kept a strict eye on her. She was so volatile and irresponsible, it was a miracle she was not caught by the Germans. I never could understand why Pemberley had passed her.

3 · Train Test

A SPY must be above all discreet. If he is loose of tongue he risks not only his own neck but the lives of others and the success of his mission. A good spy has a passion for anonymity. At the SAB (Selection Assessment Board) at Pemberley we tested men for this quality by the Train Test.

The Conducting Officer would assemble his half-dozen candidates at Waterloo for the trip to Pemberley. On British trains most coaches are divided into private compartments. As he was hustling and bustling his men into the compartments and telling them where to sit and where to put their baggage, two of us MTO's (Military Testing Officers) would come up and greet him effusively.

"Jack, old boy, how are you? We haven't seen you in ages. Hope you've been all right? I say, you do lead a strenuous life."

"Hello, Bill. Hello, Jim. Good to see you both. Cheerful as always. I've been hoping to run into you and talk about old times. Say, let's get together for a drink at the Pig and Whistle this Wednesday. Can you make it?"

"Of course, Jack. Let's make it at noon. We'll be there. Can we help with the baggage?"

"No thanks, everything's taken care of. Just a minute while I finish tidying up."

We had no set speeches, but that was roughly how the conversation would go. We took care to be overheard by the candidates. Jack, the Conducting Officer, managed to arrange it so that his men were in two different compartments, and Jim and I casually found ourselves seats, one in each compartment. Jack introduced us as old friends of his, giving the impression that the three of us were quite chummy. Then he disappeared, saying he wanted to talk to a friend at the other end of the train.

Would this halo of friendliness betray the candidates into dropping their security guard? We made no effort to interrogate or embarrass them as we exchanged cigarettes and small talk on the journey. How careful would they be in talking about their private lives, where they had been trained and where they were going? Even small talk can "blow" an operation or "burn" a spy, and we kept our ears open for slips of the tongue. Sometimes we did a bit of prodding.

These men were not yet trained in security, but they had been told to keep their mouths shut, avoid talking about themselves, and try to be as inconspicuous and unglamorous as possible. Of course slips were made, but we were not inclined to judge them severely if they were honest mistakes that training could correct. We were on the lookout for the man who is temperamentally unable to keep a secret—the sort who has to talk about himself in order to build up his ego. One out of every twenty-five candidates had this failing.

In one instance I asked the candidate, who was wearing civilian clothes, "Why are you in civvies? Why aren't you in the Army?"

"If I tell you, will you promise not to tell Jack I told you?"

"Of course."

"Well," he whispered, "I'm actually a first lieutenant in the Canadian Army but I'm not in uniform, because I'm in the *BRITISH SECRET INTELLIGENCE!*"

"How very interesting," I said, and switched the topic. There was no need for more. He did not know it, but he had already flunked out of Pemberley. He was allowed to go through the four-day assessment, but immediately afterwards received orders for an "important assignment" to a paramilitary school. This school was really a holding area where indiscreet persons were allowed to cool off their knowledge while they learned noncommittal facts about weapons and radio. I don't suppose he ever knew why he was sidetracked.

Then there was the American Lieutenant, a brazen young man with a loud voice and a hostile attitude. He hardly needed any probing from me to get him to talk.

"I'm getting sick and tired of being pushed around. When O.S.S. recruited me they promised to send me to France and instead they put me on a desk job in London. Now there is more red tape and I've got to go through some damned school to see if I've got the stuff. It's a lot of bull! I'm a college graduate and I speak French fluently.

O.S.S. gets one more chance. If they snag me with red tape again, I'm going to blow my top to Drew Pearson and tell him about the red-tape artists and the phonies in O.S.S."

I tried to pipe him down but he was not even conscious of my wrinkled brow. He was a menace and the British asked O.S.S. to chill him. I think he was sent to "Siberia," an isolated post on the rainy west coast of Scotland. I wonder if he ever told Pearson?

The importance of security is shown by the experience of Charlie Garrett, a very good friend of mine who is now an oil engineer overseas. Charlie parachuted into France as a resistance organizer. The local Gestapo headquarters was planning a series of reprisals on the French villagers. Within a week after his arrival Charlie led a *coup-de-main* team in a raid on this Gestapo headquarters, and killed all the officers and men there. Then they set to work to burn all the records on the local citizens which the Gestapo had accumulated. As Charlie riffled through the files, he was startled to come upon his own folder. There it was, and he had arrived in France only a few days before. It contained his *nom-de-guerre*, his real identity, and the date of his arrival in France. Someone must have talked.

4 · Obstacles, Minefields, and Acid Baths

THE candidates arrived at Pemberley in the late afternoon and spent the rest of the day getting settled and taking paper-and-pencil tests. Next morning they began the gruelling series of Situation Tests, starting with the Individual Obstacle Course.

This course, which the candidates ran one at a time, was designed to measure physical fitness, agility and coordination, courage, alertness, and the ability to follow simple instructions. Different obstacles called for different qualities. A man with strong arms and shoulders but weak legs could concentrate on the obstacles requiring strength in arms and shoulders, and vice versa. A poorly-muscled man could try those that called for ingenuity and courage, for even if a candidate were not in good physical shape he could still earn a passing grade by using his head.

My chief duty as an MTO was to supervise the Situation Tests. When a candidate came to take the Obstacle Course I would say to him:

"Listen. These are your instructions. This is an obstacle course. Each obstacle has a sign showing its point value. The total number of points for the course is 85, but you need only 50 to pass. You decide where you want to start and which obstacles you want to do. Now I'll show you the obstacles."

I then took the man up to each obstacle, showed him its point value, and answered his questions as best I could without doing his thinking for him. After this instruction tour I would ask, "Do you have any more questions before you begin?" These questions taken care of, I would say:

"You will have fifteen minutes. Are you ready? GO!"

I made notes of the way he had behaved and the questions he had asked, and went on making notes as I watched him running the course.

Some of the obstacles were quite simple—climbing up to and through a crotch in a thick tree-trunk; making a running broad jump over a set distance; scaling a fifteen-foot wall of horizontal boards nailed together. Other obstacles required not only co-ordination and timing but also good old-fashioned guts. Many candidates did not find it easy to walk along a slack rope suspended high in air between two trees with only another slack rope overhead for handhold; or to stand on a stepladder, grab a rope, and swing themselves over a six-foot barrier; or to scale a fireman's ladder placed against a tree, climb out on a limb, and from there slide down a seventy-foot rope whose other end was fastened to the base of another tree; or to climb up a tree and walk along a plank a foot wide, twenty feet long, and twelve feet above the ground; or to climb up a crude ladder nailed to a tree-trunk, step off the ladder on a shaky platform twenty-five feet from the ground, leap out into the air to catch a rope six feet away and slide down the rope to earth. Needless to say there were occasional wrenched wrists, cracked ribs, and twisted or broken ankles.

Some men, when confronted by these obstacles, would ask to quit then and there. A professional ping-pong player, who was slated to be dropped behind the lines in his own country, held out his lily-white ladylike hands to me and complained:

"If I do what you ask me to, I may ruin my hands. I make a living with my hands."

"But you will not be allowed to go on your mission unless you at least attempt this obstacle course."

"Do I have to go?" he asked.

"Of course not," I replied.

He spent most of his remaining three days playing ping-pong. With his right hand behind his back, and using his left hand instead of a paddle, he easily beat the best of the amateur ping-pong players at Pemberley. He had a knack of putting a curve on the ball so that it would go over the net but quickly bounce back to his side before his opponent had a chance of hitting it. We wasted no more time talking of sending him on a mission.

Some impulsive, excitable souls would hurry hither and yon, rushing from obstacle to obstacle, sometimes getting lost in the thick grass and underbrush, and then shamefacedly admit that they had forgotten the instructions. Others, stodgy and slow, would dilly-dally between obstacles, brush themselves off carefully, and end up with fewer than twenty points. One middle-aged man began to walk the plank, lost his nerve, tried to crawl it, stuck halfway across, and lay belly on the board, holding on with all his strength and bleating for help.

One husky paratrooper climbed the fireman's ladder to the limb of the tree, seized the rope, and then deliberately let go. He broke his ankle. As we got him into the car to send him to the hospital he said, "I did exactly what you told me to. I hope I passed."

Another paratrooper, instead of walking the slack rope, tried doing it hand over hand with his legs dangling. He lost his grip, somersaulted to the ground, landed on his back, got up, climbed up the tree to the rope, and started the hand-over-hand stunt again. He was immensely pleased when I told him he could walk it. "Oh, that's easy," he said, as he sprinted across.

Then there was the American private who had fought in North Africa and Italy. His division was slated to hit the Normandy beaches, but O.S.S. wanted him because of his fluent French. He climbed up the ladder nailed to the treetrunk, stepped on to the shaky platform, and stood there quivering with fright, trying to screw up courage to leap out six feet to the rope. For half an hour the Conducting Officer and I stood beneath the tree and encouraged him to make the jump. It was a crucial point for him. He would go to the edge of the platform and poise his body for the jump, then shudder and back up to the tree and hug it. The Conducting Officer and I went up and jumped off to convince him there was nothing to it. He balked. We did it again. Finally he made the leap. I sent him up a second time and he did it straight away. He was so broken up that I took him back to the house. On the way I said:

"If you are afraid to make such a simple jump, how can you even hope to finish your parachute training and jump behind the lines?"

"I don't want to," he answered. "I've always been afraid of heights, but I don't want to be a coward. That's why I said 'Yes' to the O.S.S. man who asked me to join up. If I had told him I was afraid of heights, he would have thought I was yellow. I'm not afraid to hit the beach again. I'm used to the noise of bullets. I'd rather face machine-gun fire than have to do this kind of stuff."

We agreed with him that he could serve his country better by going back to his division.

The usual candidate garnered his fifty points in ten to fifteen minutes. A few failed to earn their fifty points within fifteen minutes, while the most alert and athletic finished in less than three minutes. We MTO's kept ourselves in shape by running the course every day before breakfast. We made better time than any of the candidates except one, an American decathlon champion. He, poor fellow, later broke his back in the field.

When the candidate had run the course the MTO would question him, to get at the reasons for his actions. (It was our practice to do this after each Situation Test.) "What were your instructions?" "Why did you choose the obstacles you did?" "What was your plan?" "Have you ever run an obstacle course before?" "Do you enjoy doing things like this?" "Which of the obstacles did you like best?"

"Why?" "Which of them don't you like?" "Why?" All the while the MTO was making notes of his answers and how he gave them. At the end he would be assigned a rating— 1 being complete failure and 9, superior—and escorted to the next test.

Sometimes we noticed a candidate who carefully avoided all the height-obstacles and earned his fifty points without them. If such a man was scheduled for a mission that entailed jumping out of a plane we would ask him to go back and tackle at least two height-obstacles, including the leap from the platform to the rope. If it turned out that the man had a deathly fear of heights, he was failed for that mission, unless arrangements could be made for him to go in by some other way than parachute.

A passing score on the Obstacle Course was indispensable for a man (or woman) who was going to become an active saboteur or guerrilla leader. It was possible for a man, especially an older man, to be good at organizing espionage nets without having the agility or daring needed to pass the Obstacle Course. One or two such cases were passed for espionage at Pemberley. The one I remember best was a jolly roly-poly Frenchman, fifty-two years old, who looked like the bartender in an old-time saloon. We called him The Barrel. It would have taken him months of training to earn a passing score on the Obstacle Course. He had all the will in the world but he simply wasn't fit for it. He never got as far as climbing up to the shaky platform, but if he had, his two hundred and seventy-five pounds would have brought it crashing down. There were special reasons why Headquarters were anxious to use him.

He knew Paris like the back of his hand and had thousands of contacts, and his jovial red face and rotund body did not suggest the spy. He was enormously patriotic and anxious to go back to France. They gave him a bare minimum of training, and one practice parachute jump—from a balloon so that he would not get hurt. Then he jumped into France and I heard no more of him. He probably carried out his mission successfully. As far as we at Pemberley were concerned, no news about a man in the field was good news. We heard about it soon enough, through the grapevine, when a man was killed, or muffed his job.

The Barrel was a rare exception to the rule that a spy must be versatile, particularly in wartime when the situation in the field is fluid. A man may find himself a courier spy one day and a guerrilla captain the next. It is a basic principle that a spy must not be only a specialist but an all-round man, a kind of decathlon champion in intelligence.

After the Individual Obstacle Course came the Minefield and Acid Bath Tests. These called for imagination and resourcefulness, qualities essential in a spy, who may often find himself in a tight corner.

In the Minefield Test, the candidate was shown a plot of land twenty feet square and one foot higher than the surrounding soil. The MTO told him:

"This plot of land is a minefield. Mines and booby traps are hidden below the surface. It is an extremely dangerous area, but you must get across it somehow in fifteen minutes, without going around either side."

There was a horizontal wooden bar fifteen feet above the minefield, stretching from the left to the right side. An observant candidate would also notice a fairly substantial rope lying amid a pile of sticks and stones on his side of the minefield. All he had to do was toss one end of the rope over the bar and catch it as it swung back, knot both ends of the rope securely together, gauge how high up he would have to grasp the rope to avoid hitting the minefield in his swing, and then swing himself across.

Most of the candidates saw the point of the rope and bar, and swung across without much trouble. But some behaved oddly. They would zigzag across the minefield on tiptoes. "By zigzagging I may avoid the mines, and by walking on my toes I won't be so heavy as to explode them." Others would hide behind a tree and throw rocks and pebbles into the minefield in the hope of detonating the mines. A few athletes climbed up the rope to the bar, stood on it, and jumped to the far side of the minefield. They did it the hard way.

Immediately afterwards came the Acid Bath Test. We showed the candidate to a rectangular pool of water twenty feet long by ten feet wide and six inches deep, and told him:

"Here is a pool of sulphuric acid. This acid is very dangerous and will burn you badly if it touches your skin. You must start from here and somehow get to the other end of the pool without going around the edge. You have fifteen minutes."

If the candidate searched around he would find three logs, each about a foot long and eight inches thick, with smooth ends. They were weatherbeaten and camouflaged among the shrubbery near the pool. He could not find them simply by gazing. He had to feel for them with his hands and feet and then dislodge them. Then he could use them as movable stepping stones by placing them on end in the water, standing on two and pushing the third ahead for the next step, and repeating the process until he reached the far end of the pool.

About one man in four failed the Acid Bath Test, because he never bothered to look for the "tools" with which to solve the problem. Some would find one or two logs and look no further. With only one log the crossing could not be made. With two logs the crossing could be made, but very slowly, since the candidate had to stand with both feet on one log while he pushed the other log ahead. This required a great deal of effort, as well as poise and nimbleness. Often the candidate would lose his balance and topple off into the muddy water.

One man who failed the Acid Bath was a high-ranking executive in a multi-billion-dollar American corporation. He raced back and forth on the path leading to the pool, muttered, cursed, searched here and there but never found the logs. At last he growled, "This is a damn' fool test," stepped into the "acid"—soaking sneakers, socks and feet, and walked the length of the pool. He was the same in other tests, too—easily irritated, obsessed by haste, and incapable of seeing more than one way of doing anything. Even in the problems he did solve, he wasted a great deal of energy.

Some of the candidates reminded me of Köhler's chimpanzees. Professor Köhler is an eminent psychologist who has carried out a number of experiments on the reasoning powers of the great apes. He used to put his chimps in a cage where there was a bunch of bananas hanging just out of reach, and several boxes on the floor. Some of the chimps had the sense to move a box under the bananas and stand on it, but others jumped on the boxes where they stood and grabbed wildly in the air, nowhere near the bananas.

The solution of the Acid Bath problem could be reached by different approaches. A systematic thinker would propose various solutions to himself and discard them, talking aloud as he walked about looking for something that might suggest the answer. A man who relied more on intuition might find the logs, handle them, try them this way and that, before hitting on the right use for them. A few candidates found the logs but never could think what to do with them. But as a rule if a man had got hold of the logs —or the rope, in the Minefield Test—and kept on handling them even in an aimless fashion, after a while he would give a sudden start and cry *"Aha!"* or *"I got it!"* This kind of sudden insight is what we psychologists rather pompously call, "the aha phenomenon." These two problems, the Minefield and the Acid Bath, were really quite simple, but by watching how a man set about solving them we could form a notion of how he would attack other problems. As a general rule a candidate's working methods in later, more complex Situation Tests were basically the same as in the Minefield and the Acid Bath.

5 · Groupstacle

THE situation tests had each a particular purpose and were given in a fixed order. The three I have just described were individual tests in which the candidate had to rely entirely on his own resources. Next came the Groupstacle (Group Obstacle Course), which called for team as well as muscle work. The six men in a group ran the course together.

The aim of the Groupstacle was to find how far each man would or could (1) assume leadership in a group, (2) contribute ideas for solving a problem, (3) co-operate with others, (4) do his share of the dirty work.

Before they started, the MTO would take them over the course and explain it to them. On the ground lay a ten-foot log weighing eighty pounds. First they had to get the log and themselves over a ten-foot brick wall. Then they had to carry the log two hundred yards downhill to where a heavy, dirty tarpaulin was stretched on the ground. They had to crawl under this tarpaulin and drag the log with them. The next obstacle, two hundred yards further on, was a tree with a bough jutting out, twenty feet above the ground. Two ropes were lying at the foot of the tree. The group had to get the log, but not themselves, over this bough and then carry the log twenty yards to the brink of a deep, muddy stream. They had to cross and get the log across from a small platform on one side of the stream to another platform on the other side. The distance between the two platforms, nine and a half feet, had been carefully calculated to make it just less than the length of the log and just too wide for a standing broad jump. It was impossible to take a running broad jump from the tiny platform.

"When all of you and the log are safely across this stream, the problem is finished," the MTO told them. "Now let's go back up to the hill where we left the log." When they reached the top of the hill he would ask, "Do you want to discuss it before you begin? Let me know when you're ready to start."

The MTO was, as always, jotting down notes in his little book. Who were trying to get the lead? Who were hanging back? Who came forward with a plan? Were rival cliques forming? When they announced they were all ready to start he would say:

"The record for this course is four minutes and sixteen seconds. We want you to try to beat it. Ready? GO!"

This is how the best teams ran the course: Three men helped one another to the top of the wall. The three men left on the ground pushed the log up to the three on the wall. They threw it over and then helped the three on the ground to climb the wall. Even before the last man reached the top, the two who were first over the wall were running downhill to the tarpaulin with the log on their shoulders. Two others overtook them, crawled under the tarpaulin and ran on to the tree. The last two men caught up with the log-bearers and held up the tarpaulin while the log-bearers crawled under it, pushing the log. Then the last two crawled under the tarpaulin, overtook the log-bearers again, ran on to the tree, and heaved a rope to the first two men who by now were straddling the branch. When the log arrived, the log-bearers had a chance to get their breath while the two men waiting tied the end of the rope to the log and the two men on the branch pulled it up and heaved it over. Then logs, ropes, and men went on to the platform at the edge of the stream. There was only just room for them all. The men tied one rope to each end of the log, stood it on end, and dropped it neatly across to the other platform, with just three inches to spare on either side. Then they straddled or ran over it to the far platform, the last man taking the end of the rope with him. Then the log was yanked over by both ropes.

This test was always very exciting to watch. Emotions ran high, and cries of *merde* and worse rent the air. As soon as they had finished, the MTO would say, "You have run the course in —— minutes and —— seconds. Now discuss among yourselves how you might have done it better. Take no notice of me."

If the team had worked well together and made good time they would hug each other and slap each other on the back. But if they were dissatisfied with their performance they fell to bickering, name-calling, and even fist fights. I especially enjoyed the French teams. They attacked the problem with tremendous enthusiasm, good humor, and camaraderie. When things went wrong they would shout violent abuse at one another. If Englishmen or Americans had exchanged those insults they would never have been able to speak to one another again, but the French, an hour or so later, had wiped the slate and were the best of friends again. Sometimes their love of laughter got the better of them and they would be so entertained by the antics of some member of the group that the will to win would evaporate.

The Groupstacle could not be solved, even in forty-five minutes, unless the group was able to form a concerted plan of action and stick to it, or an effective leader emerged to take control. A hostile faction would frustrate an excellent plan by giving contrary instructions. Or two leaders would fight for control of the group. Or one of the men pushing the log up to the wall would fancy himself insulted, throw the log down and shout, "If that's how you're going to talk to me you can take this log and shove it." He had to have an apology before he would pitch in again. Or the bearer at one end of the log would discover that the other man was not carrying his fair share of the weight and would drop his end of the log with, "Now you try to carry it yourself for a while!" If the plan went awry at the stream, the log often fell into the water. Unless it was tied at both ends it could not be pulled out, but most likely one of the men fell in after it and scrambled out on the bank covered with mire. Friendships formed or animosities aroused in running the course often lasted throughout the rest of the candidates' stay at Pemberley.

Too many clever and dominant figures in a group were apt to compete for leadership and disrupt group action. On the contrary, there were groups where no one emerged as a leader but all worked beautifully as a team and ran the course in fast time. Often the leaderless team consisted of weak members with low ratings on individual tests, but in a group they were effective above the level of their separate abilities. This was real democracy in action.

Such teams were often Polish. The Poles combined tremendous group loyalty with a deep suspicion of authority. When taking paper-and-pencil tests they would walk around and look at one another's papers and resist attempts to make them go back to their seats. I was always sorry for the psychologist when he had a Polish group to test. When the Poles did quarrel among themselves it was usually about the tanks. The Russians had offered a number of tanks to General Anders and his Polish forces, to be used in the fight against the Germans. The Poles who came to Pemberley were being selected, many of them, to learn how to operate and repair tanks. Then they were to parachute into Poland and take over the tanks. Most of them were inclined to reason that they should use the tanks to fight the Russians, who were more bitter enemies than the Germans. I don't know what happened in the end. I know that these men did go into Poland. I suppose they ultimately fought with the Russians against the Germans and they may be sorry for it now, if they are still alive.

The successful leaderless teams were not very common. Usually a leader emerged. A good leader had to be both a thinker and a boss. He had to make a workable plan and induce the others to accept it. In one group there was a strange leader—the body and temperament of one man combined with the brain of another.

Bernie was a skinny boy in his early twenties, son of a wealthy Brooklyn manufacturer. He had had a French nursery governess and had then been to school and college in France. His French was perfect. O.S.S. had picked him up as a private in the U.S. Army in the hope that he could be sent to France as an agent. He had an excellent brain, but the face of a submissive squirrel and a wheezy, complaining voice. He was always carping and finding fault. He had been the butt of the group from the moment they assembled at Waterloo Station. In the Groupstacle when he made suggestions he was either openly sneered at or pointedly ignored by the others. All but Moxie.

Moxie was a burly, swarthy Frenchman nearing forty with the body of a weight-lifter, the voice of a stevedore, and the manner of a Fort Benning infantry sergeant. He had been a black-marketeer in Paris, but when some of his deals were made in favor of resistance groups, the Nazis began reaching for his scalp and he fled across the Pyrenees. The hope was that he could be trained in clandestine intelligence, return to Paris and there resume his criminal affiliations, to his own advantage and that of the Allies. Moxie was not only illiterate; tests showed him to be not too far above the level of a high-grade moron in respect to abstract intelligence. But he was astute, cunning, and forceful. He alone of the group was shrewd enough to realise that Bernie's ideas could be put to good use.

From the beginning of the Groupstacle the Parisian black-marketeer appropriated the boy from Brooklyn. He suggested that they work together. Bernie would tell Moxie what to do and Moxie would give the orders and see that they were carried out. The result was that the team completed the course in very fast time. The two worked together in the same way on all the later group tests. We were so impressed by this remarkable pair that we recommended they go into the field together. When we found that this could not be arranged, because O.S.S. wanted Bernie and de Gaulle wanted Moxie, we made it a condition of Moxie's passing the assessment that he should only be sent into Paris along with another specially picked "brain." For all I know he is working the Paris black market today.

6 · The Pond

ᒣᒧᒣᒧᒣᒧᒣᒧᒣᒧᒣᒧᒣᒧᒣᒧᒣᒧᒣᒧᒣᒧᒣᒧ

THERE was a pond on the Pemberley estate with a tiny island in the middle. We took the candidates in a group to the edge of the pond, pointed to a square wooden box lying on the ground, and told them:

"Here is a box which contains very delicate radio equipment. It weighs more than a hundred pounds. If the box is dropped, or if it gets wet, the equipment will be ruined. It is your job to get this box safely over to the island. You must all get over to the island, too, without getting yourselves wet. If you get wet you will be failed and have to drop out of the problem. Remember, the box must not be dropped and it must not get wet. Do it any way you want to. These are your only instructions. You will have one half-hour."

We made the rule that the candidates must not get wet because we had to put them through other problems afterwards. In any case, the pond was too deep to walk across.

We had strewn various ropes, pulleys, poles, and sticks along the shores of the pond. We had also hidden a wobbly raft behind a clump of bushes at the edge of the water.

The raft was made of boards kept afloat by two empty oil drums which were unevenly placed so that the raft tipped over easily. On the far side of the pond we had hidden a much better raft, really firmly built. This steady raft could not be found without a complete reconnaissance of the shore.

The wobbly raft would not support one man for the journey to the island even without the extra hundred pounds of the radio box. The steady raft would easily support one man and the box, and he could punt across to the island with a pole. Another system was to set up a rope pulley between trees on the shore and on the island. Either way the problem could not be solved without the steady raft.

In each group there was usually a loud, boisterous, eager beaver. He would find the wobbly raft and shout:

"Hey, fellows, I've got the answer. Here's a raft. They hid it behind the bushes here. I'll pull it along and we'll get the box over that way."

"But will it support the box?" another man would ask.

"Oh yes, I'm sure of that."

"How do you know?"

"I'll show you," and he would jump upon the raft. Since it was ill-balanced and he landed on one side, the raft quickly turned somersault and the eager beaver got a ducking. In winter the water was almost freezing and would quickly sober him up.

Most of the candidates who fell off the raft had the sense to go straight back to the house and change their clothes. They were out of the game anyway. But one man came and stood passively by my side. It was January. He was drenched, shaking with cold, his teeth rattling in his head. It was against the rules for me to speak to him. I waited for him to go, but he still stood there shivering. I was afraid he might die of pneumonia so at last I said, "Why don't you go up to the house and change and meet us in the woods for the next problem?" "Oh, thank you, thank you," he said as if I had just told him he wasn't going to be hanged today after all. His meek dejection after he fell in and got wet was a sorry contrast to his noisy self-assurance at the start of the problem.

There were candidates who not only disregarded our instructions but so bungled the problem that it became a fiasco for the whole group. One of these was a paratrooper, a man of great daring, but so self-centered, irritable, and cocky, that he was a constant annoyance to the others. He fell off the wobbly raft and refused to listen to his teammates who ruled, correctly, that he was disqualified. Instead he swam out to a sandbar halfway across to the island and bullied the others into throwing one end of the rope to him. Then he tried to make them suspend the heavy box of radio equipment on the rope while he served as the other end of the pulley. It was so silly that the rest of the group lost patience and quit. When he realized he could not win he began to clown, paddling round and round the pond and waving and yelling at the others. He seemed determined to ruin the problem for them when he found he could not shine as the leader.

The Pond test was not for prima donnas. Concerted planning and effort were needed. The best groups would discuss various possible solutions first, sometimes for as long as ten or fifteen minutes, before embarking on a definite course of action. The two most common reasons for failure were: (1) The group did not make a complete search and never found the stable raft. Failing with the shaky raft, they looked no further. Or (2) they worked by trial and error, never forming a logical plan but listening to the men who happened to yell the loudest.

This problem was rarely completed in the half-hour allowed, but it gave very valuable information. It was a real problem, full of pitfalls and stumbling blocks and requiring close team-work. I often thought it should be called the Snafu Test, because it showed a candidate's reaction to a series of failures. At the end of the half-hour we called the group together and asked them what their plan had been and how they might have done better. Sometimes a timid, thoughtful soul would give us the perfect solution. He had known it all the time but nobody had heard him amid the shouting. We often see this happen in everyday life, where a man with good ideas will lack the strength of personality to get them accepted, while a forceful, dominant fellow is busily putting across ideas that are worthless.

Before we leave the Pond, I must tell you about our star team. They were eight Frenchmen, recruited in North Africa, who had already completed a number of missions in the field. This team came to Pemberley partly as a sport for them between missions and partly because we wanted to see a really top-notch performance against which to measure the performance of the candidates. This team was superb on every test. It was a pleasure to watch them. They finished the Pond well ahead of time and filled in the rest of the half-hour by swimming about in the nude, imitating porpoises, going over or under each other.

The leader stood about five and a half feet and weighed at least a hundred and ninety pounds, most of it solid muscle. All of them were tremendously strong, fiercely competitive, genial ruffians. In the field they were a completely independent group, responsible only to themselves for the completion of their assigned missions. They even had their own doctor, one of the team members. Their work was chiefly sabotage and demolitions against French munition factories working for the Germans. Once when they were taking the Pyrenees route into France, they had to take their suitcases into the custom house for inspection. The first Frenchman opened his bag. "Personal possessions only," he said. The customs officer lifted up the layer of clothing on top and revealed pistols, grenades, and plastic explosives. He looked up in amazement, his mouth open and ready to speak. But the Frenchmen had made a circle around him, and he noticed that one was pointing a pistol straight at his belly. "Ah yes, of course, personal possessions," the customs officer said hastily as he snapped the bag shut and, with a bow and a flourish, waved them all through.

7 · The Barbed-Wire Barrier

ЛЛЛЛЛЛЛЛЛЛЛЛЛЛЛЛЛЛЛЛ

THE barbed-wire barrier was another group problem. I led the group of candidates to a road which was blocked by a barbed-wire barrier six feet high and six feet thick, and gave them these instructions:

"You have been out on a reconnaissance in German-held territory. You are now on your way back to your own headquarters but you are stopped by this barbed-wire barrier. It is electrically charged. You have no way of going around it because it completely blocks the road. The Germans are after you, and you must get across within twenty minutes. You may use any tools or any means you like to get across this barrier, but don't forget that it is electrically charged. If you even touch it you will be electrocuted. You are here alone. We MTO's are really not present at all and cannot advise you."

Close at hand stood a tree with branches projecting as far as the barrier but not overhanging it. Ropes and sticks and logs and planks, plenty of them, were lying about on the ground. One way of crossing the barrier was to tie a rope to the outer end of a branch, hold the other end of the rope while standing on a lower branch near the tree trunk, let go, and be carried over the barrier by the pendulum swing. The only man who did this lost the seat of his pants on the way.

Another method was to tie two planks together with ropes to form an X. Two men would hold the X upright and a third plank was placed horizontally in the crotch of the X so as to project out at an angle over the barrier. The two men would hold the plank in place in the crotch while a third walked the plank and jumped across the barbed wire to the other side.

A variation of this method was to place a plank on the shoulders of two men instead of on two crossed planks. Either the man nearest the barrier was considerably taller than the other man or he made himself taller by standing on a platform of boards. Otherwise the plank would not tilt up enough to clear the barrier.

Obviously the last two men would not cross in this way. The men who had already crossed over would tie a rope to the end of a board and tilt the board up over the barrier from their side. One at a time the two remaining men would grab the rope and their team-mates would hoist-jerk them over the barrier, as if landing a fish. We did not see this very often, for the groups seldom had time to finish in the twenty minutes allowed.

This was a problem in which men could get hurt, either by accident or by design. There was one candidate who was detested by the others in his group. They chose to cross the barrier by balancing a plank on the shoulders of two men. Just as the unpopular man was poised for the jump from the end of the plank, the two men supporting it relaxed their hold a little. He missed his footing, and jumped right into the middle of the barbed wire, which tore into his flesh. His team-mates roared with sadistic laughter and made no attempt to help him out but went on as if nothing had happened. When the five of them were all across the barrier one man looked at his watch, then pointed at the man in the barbed wire and said, "Look, he's still alive. We have only two minutes left and we don't have enough time to get him out, so we'll just have to leave him here and go on our way."

Another said, "No, he'll talk and tell the Germans all about us."

"Let's kill him," urged a third. "Then we'll be sure he won't talk."

So one of them came close to the barrier, pointed his index finger at the man's head, and said, "BANG! BANG!"

Just then time was up. I made them help me to extricate the poor fellow and get him to the hospital.

You may feel that a problem like this is too cruel and dangerous to use in a selection program. It is well to remember that men going into enemy territory are exposed to far greater hazards than this. If they are faint-hearted, or if they are the sort who make themselves hated in a group, it might just as well be discovered before they go into the field and are hurt by something worse than barbed wire.

8 · The Criminal-Gang Problem

A SPY must, of course, be loyal and devoted to his country. He must be, in the deepest sense, a man of integrity. But he has to be adaptable. Just as an infantry soldier shoots the enemy soldier so should the spy have no hesitation if, in the line of duty, he has to do away with someone who is a threat to him and his country. In other words, although he is a man of integrity, he must be able to lie, cheat, and murder. A man whose private scruples will not allow him to behave like a criminal, even in his country's interests, is not cut out for a spy.

To find out whether our candidates had this sort of adaptability we set up the Criminal Gang problem. This problem also tested the candidate's reaction to extreme danger and intense frustration. I would lead the candidate to a remote staircase in a secluded wing of the huge, rambling mansion which housed the SAB at Pemberley and tell him:

"You are a member of a criminal gang. I am a hotel-owner, the proprietor of the hotel we are in now. I have given your gang shelter, protection, and help. I am loyal, absolutely loyal, and I am implicated in the crimes of your gang. The chief of the gang had an office in an attic room in this hotel. The other day police came here in search of him. I warned him and he fled. They did not find his attic office. I managed to divert them. When the chief escaped he took with him all compromising papers —all but one. Somewhere in the attic the chief left behind a list of the names and addresses of all members of the gang. He has sent you here to search the attic, find the list, and take it away with you. He has also told you to take away any other papers or objects that may identify or implicate anybody associated with the gang. Don't worry about being captured. I am here, and I will give you ample warning if anything should happen. Now let's go to the attic. I'll show you where it is." Then I would drop the role of hotel-owner for a moment and say in my normal voice, "There is a Military Testing Officer in the attic. Take no notice of him; he is only an observer."

I then showed the candidate to the attic office on the third floor. Before showing him in, I would answer, in my character of hotel-owner, any honest questions he raised and give him last-minute assurances if needed.

The attic office which he entered was a dark and dreary place right underneath the slanting roof, with barely room to stand up in. There were no windows and the only light came from a dim electric bulb hanging by a cord from the ceiling. Beneath the light was a makeshift desk, a cabinet topped by a marble slab. On one side of the cabinet were two doors, each enclosing a set of shelves. There was also a third storage section which could only be reached by lifting up the marble slab. In a corner of the attic was a battered bookcase stacked with old newspapers. There was a chair with the stuffing sticking out of the seat and another chair with only three legs. The fourth leg was lying on the floor. The cabinet contained a copy of André Maurois' book *Why France Fell*, an old comb with some teeth missing, a rusty nail-file, and an empty coin purse. We always rearranged the attic room in exactly the same way, however much the candidate had mussed it up.

I did not enter the room with the candidate but stood outside. In the room the observer MTO was standing in a corner, pad and pencil in hand, scribbling a record. If the candidate spoke to him he made no reply but merely jotted down the remark made to him.

Some peered into every nook and cranny of the dark attic as though looking for an unwanted guest. Others began searching the room but kept going back to try the door to make sure they hadn't been locked in. Some worked as calmly and quietly as if browsing in a secondhand bookstore. Others would talk to themselves, either speaking their thoughts aloud or just rattling on out of nervousness. One man carefully unfolded the newspapers one by one, looked through each one, and when he found nothing carefully refolded them and put them back on the shelf just as they had been, then impulsively rushed back, went through them again in a hurry and left them scattered about the room. One man picked up the three-legged chair, bottom side up, scrutinized every inch of it, explored it all over with his fingers; then went to the other chair and pulled out the seat stuffing; then unscrewed the electric bulb, struck a match, and looked into the bulb socket. Another man picked up the comb and ran it through his hair; cleaned his nails with the rusty nail-file; picked up the book by Maurois, leafed through it, then sat down and read a number of pages, all the while murmuring "Oh, Oh, Oh." I asked him afterwards why he had done all these things and all he could answer was, "I don't know."

Some men had a plan of procedure or at least seemed purposeful in their approach. They carefully and systematically investigated the places where the list of gang members was likely to be hidden. Other harried creatures would examine the book, then the stuffing in the chair, then the newspapers, then the stuffing again; peer outside the door; return to the newspapers; open one of the doors in the cabinet and close it without looking inside; open the other door and glance inside without feeling into the dark corners; shrug their shoulders and continue looking in a confused, random fashion.

As a rule the candidate went first to the cabinet which had been arranged as the most conspicuous object in the room. It was in the cabinet that we had placed the list of gang members. There was a decoy envelope and a real envelope, each with "List" written on the outside. The decoy envelope was in the left shelf section and contained only a blank sheet of paper. The real envelope was in the top section under the marble slab. Sometimes a candidate would stuff the decoy envelope into his pocket without looking at it and dash out of the room in the belief that his mission was accomplished. Usually, however, he would look inside the envelope and either put it back in the cabinet or put it in his pocket and keep on looking. Those who kept the decoy envelope explained later that they didn't know why they had taken it, or else that the writing might be in invisible ink.

The candidate had fifteen minutes in which to find the real envelope. As soon as he found it we started the second phase of the problem. If at the end of fifteen minutes he still had not found the real envelope we started the second phase anyway. The MTO observer in the room would give me the signal while I stood outside in the corridor. His signal was to cough and then at once clear his throat. While the candidate was searching the room the MTO had already coughed and cleared his throat several times so that the candidate would attach no special meaning to the sounds, but he did not clear his throat immediately after a cough until he was ready to give me the come-on signal.

Upon hearing the signal I would come running down the corridor in a state of great excitement, and as I opened the door of the attic office I would exclaim, "The police are here. Quick, quick, follow me!" The candidate was almost always frightened or at least unnerved. The very noise of my running would sometimes so alarm him that when I flung open the door of the room he was crouching behind the desk or trying to hide behind the observer MTO.

This situation was designed to find among other things

whether the candidate would panic. Most of them would drop everything and dash wildly after me. Others rushed out, rushed back again to pick up something they had dropped or forgotten, and rushed out again. A few made sure to pick up the real envelope and a few other things that might possibly be incriminating, calmly tidied up the room, and then followed me down the corridor. I would lead the candidate round the bend of the corridor to a window, grab his arm, and tell him in a low, urgent voice:

"The way to get out is through this window on to the roof. Go down that rope ladder to the second-floor roof, there you'll find a rope down to the first-floor roof, and from there you can get down to the ground by a downspout. Hide in the woods across the road. I'll look for you there."

Quite often the candidate had opened the window and was halfway out, intent on making his getaway without stopping to listen to my instructions, and I would have to pull him back. Just before I let him go I would calm down a bit and say reassuringly, "Don't worry. Everything is all right. The police have just arrived in the lobby and I can keep them talking there for at least five minutes. So if you haven't finished the job you can go back and do it if you want to. You will have at least five more minutes."

Only one out of eight candidates took advantage of the chance to return to the attic office. The others didn't care to run any more risks or else they were too excited to listen.

When the candidate was out on the roof he would sometimes forget my instructions and run around like a cat in a strange puzzle box or come peering in at the attic windows. When it was snowing or raining a man might slip on the rope ladder or the rope and sprain his ankle. Luckily no one ever fell off the third-floor roof, but on several occasions men on the first-floor roof failed to find the rain gutter and jumped to the ground or tried to climb down by the ivy, which would not bear their weight.

As soon as the candidate reached the ground he was met by the MTO who had observed him in the attic. The MTO first told him to hand over everything he had removed from the attic office. Some men had taken everything they could stuff in their pockets and shirt fronts. As each object was handed over, the MTO would ask, "Why did you take this?" After this, he would ask other questions, such as: "Why didn't you bring the list of the gang members?" "Why did you turn down the chance of five minutes' extra search?" "What were your instructions?" "If you had a plan, what was it?" The MTO seldom criticized a candidate's performance, and then only to gain a better understanding of the man.

This problem was given an odd twist by one candidate, a husky French paratrooper. On this occasion I was the observer MTO in the attic, and the part of the hotel-owner was played by another MTO, an Englishman who had lived many years in France. The Frenchman succeeded in finding the real envelope without much trouble. I gave the cough-and-clear-throat signal and the hotel-owner came pounding along the corridor, opened the door, and yelled his warning: "Les gendarmes sont arrivés. Vite. Vite. Suivez moi!"

The Frenchman wheeled around to face the hotel-owner, and while doing so crammed the list of the gang members into his hip pocket, then dashed blindly towards the door, and hit his forehead smack against the doorjamb. Then as the hotel-owner turned left down the corridor the Frenchman turned right. I was still standing in my corner in the attic office when, within a minute, I saw the hotel-owner go dashing down the other end of the corridor in search of the Frenchman. He found him hiding in one of the small rooms at that end, cursed him roundly for not following his instructions, and then padded back down the corridor with the Frenchman at his heels. The hotel-owner went straight on past the door of the attic office, but the Frenchman ducked into the room, glanced at me, put his fingers to his lips and breathed "Sh-h-h!" and crouched down behind the cabinet. Next moment the hotel-owner was back with, "I've lost the son-of-a-bitch again." I rolled my eyes to let him know where the Frenchman was. The hotel-owner dragged him out again and cursed him again, most abusively, for not following instructions. The Frenchman said, "I promise you, so help me God, this time I will follow you just exactly as you say. Go, and I will follow."

They went off, but in a minute the hotel-owner was back. "Damn it all, I've lost him again."

"Well," I said, "he followed you left out of the room and then you went where?"

"I went left again."

The only other branch of the corridor led to a single room. From the window there was a sheer drop of three floors to the ground. If the man had jumped he would certainly not have been able to get up and walk away, and there was no sign of him on the ground. We decided that he must have grabbed the rain gutter above the window and climbed onto the roof. We borrowed a ladder, and climbed up onto the roof to look for him. It is not easy to search a roof with so many gables. We finally found him between two of the gables, in the very middle of the roof.

"What the hell are you doing up here?" I asked.

He was amazingly logical about it all.

"This hotel-owner claims to be my friend," he said, "but any friend who shouts a warning to me in such a loud voice is obviously trying to double-cross me. He wants to let the police know where I am. I made up my mind not to believe a word he said, and not to follow any advice he gave me. I felt sure it would lead me straight into the hands of the police."

I gave him a superior rating.

We were constantly modifying the tests in use with the purpose of making them less structured—that is, more flexible. The freer the choice given to the candidate in solving the problem, the better the indication of his character and capabilities. It is easier to judge a man fairly when he is given room to reveal himself and his particular methods of attacking a problem. I am describing the tests which seem to me the most interesting and revealing from a psychological point of view. There were many others in use and we were always devising new ones. Some were disappointments.

We badly needed an alternative to the Criminal Gang so we thought up another which we called "Caught in the Act." In this problem the candidate was breaking open a footlocker to get some documents when he was surprised by two armed men (MTO's). In real life there would be a hand-to-hand fight and at least one man would be hurt, and that's just what happened in our problem. It was too realistic altogether and we discarded it in a hurry before anyone was seriously injured.

But our most spectacular failure was the Emergency Situation problem. Two candidates were stationed in ditches, one on each side of a road. A hundred yards or so further on stood a small shack.

"You are out on a reconnaissance and you have come upon an enemy outpost." Here the MTO pointed to the shack. "In there is the Communication Center of the local Gestapo. You must bring back as much information about it as you possibly can."

Just then one of our sergeants dressed up as a Gestapo officer dashed out of the shack and raced down the road towards the two candidates, apparently without seeing them.

"What are you going to do now?" asked the MTO.

The nearer candidate picked up a stout stick that was lying in the ditch and gave the Gestapo officer, as he went running by, such a clout on the back of the neck that he was knocked sprawling on his face in the road. It was the first and last time we ran that problem.

9 · Chief and Recruit

ALL the situation tests I have described so far, except the Train Test, called for a certain degree of muscular agility. A spy must also be verbally agile, able to think quickly with his tongue as well as his arms and legs. Words are often the weapons he uses to induce others to risk their lives. If he aspires to be the organizer of a spy chain and not merely a lone wolf operative, he must also be warm in his relations with others and receptive to new ideas.

One of the methods we used to estimate these important verbal-social traits was the Group Discussion, an informal gathering of the six candidates in a group to discuss topics of their own choosing. This method has since the war been widely adopted by Government and business for the selection of various types of executives and supervisors. It has been the subject of dozens of research studies, some of them by the Civil Service Commission. Since the Group Discussion has received so much attention and is now fairly well known, I am not going to talk about it. Instead I should like to describe another test we used at Pemberley to appraise these verbal-social traits. So far as I know, the Chief and Recruit problem has not been described before.

The candidate was given a printed card with these instructions:

"You are the chief of a resistance organization in France. You are known only by an alias, and only your principal agents see you in person. One of these agents has recently recruited a college student who has agreed to leave his studies and go to another part of France to work for your organization. There is no doubt of his allegiance to France and to the Resistance. He is loyal and obedient and he wants to do his best. Usually you do not see these subagents, but since this young man is a most promising worker, the agent who recruited him has asked you to talk with him and fire him with the spirit of the Resistance. You have agreed to spend ten minutes with him and to answer any questions he may raise. You are using this room as an office for the interview. You are the boss. The two MTO's in the room are observers. Pay no attention to them. Assume they are not here. Now read these instructions again and prepare for the interview. The recruit will knock on your door in about eight minutes."

No further instructions were given to the candidate. If he asked questions I would shrug my shoulders and say, "You are the boss."

There were a number of questions in my mind as I watched each chief interview the recruit. Was the chief warm and friendly, able to inspire a follower and win his trust? Or was he a cold fish? Did he put the recruit at ease, or bully and dictate to him? Did he give the recruit a chance to talk or did he merely harangue him? In answering the recruit's questions was he sensible and open-minded, trying to get facts on which to base a suggestion, or were his answers rigid and stereotyped?

The recruit was played by a sergeant dressed in civilian clothes. This sergeant had an M.A. in psychology and a flair for dramatics, and would vary his part according to the behavior of the chief. If the chief offered him a cigarette he would smoke. If the chief encouraged him to talk he would talk discreetly. If the chief bullied him he would become quiet and submissive. If the chief had a sense of humor he would chuckle along with him. During the interview he would slip in a few test questions. Here are three of the test questions along with some of the answers actually given to them by different chiefs.

"What shall I tell my parents before I leave home?"

(a) "Tell them nothing—nothing—nothing. Just leave home and forget them."

(b) "You and the agent who recruited you should arrange your cover. We will help you as much as we can in making your story so natural that it will arouse no interest."

(c) "Please tell me more about your parents."

"What shall I do about my girl friend? She loves me very much."

(a) "Forget her. Women are dangerous in the Resistance. If she asks questions, slap her face."

(b) "If you love her, marry her, swear her to secrecy, and take her along."

(c) "What do *you* think would be the best thing to do?"
"*Will I have a chance to see you again?*"
(a) "No, never again."
(b) "As often as you wish."
(c) "Perhaps, but it depends on the problems you and I must solve. In this work we avoid too many meetings in order to protect each other. One of the contact agents will speak for you to me and for me to you, but in an emergency, for the Cause, you may always come to me."

This problem was excellent for revealing sagacity and skill, or lack of them, in dealing with human beings face to face. There were many types of chief—the ponderous and dull, the warm-hearted but weak, the arrogant and self-centered, the kindly master, the cruel authoritarian, the helpful Christian.

Most chiefs were a trifle nervous but put forth their very best. Some stammered and broke down. We suffered with them as they writhed in efforts to express themselves. One poor chap, a Frenchman, said nothing for four minutes, not a word. The recruit sat there and looked at him, and he looked from the recruit to us and back again. His lips were moving, he was "speaking," but his lips and tongue produced no sound. After a long, long time he exploded,

"Help me! Help me! I can't stand this. May I go?"

As I left the room with him he said, "I want to work with my hands," and held out a pair of beautifully strong and muscular hands. Later he became a splendid worker on a sabotage team blowing up railroads and bridges.

In another session the chief was an American lieutenant.

He read his instructions and sat down behind the desk. The recruit knocked on the door, which was slightly ajar. The chief gestured to him to come in and sit down and he did so, shutting the door behind him. The chief did not speak. He gritted his teeth, he clamped his jaw, his breathing became heavy and quick, his face flushed red and then paled, beads of sweat broke out on his forehead. After a few minutes of this he turned to me and gasped, "Would you mind opening the door just a bit?" I opened it, and the chief then regained control of himself and made a good showing on the problem. When it was over he said to me:

"Strange thing. I guess you'd call it claustrophobia. I can explain it, but I can't do anything about it. Life at home was rough. My father was brutal. I looked older than my age, seemed to be about sixteen or seventeen when I was twelve. I ran away from home, but the police picked me up when I was riding the rails. I wouldn't tell them where I came from, so they *locked me up. I was in jail almost a week.* I never did tell them. They thought I was a thief. I was deadly afraid of telling them where my home was. My father would have beat me to a pulp. Ever since then I can't bear staying in a room where the door is shut. I get panicky."

Like any other skilled workman the spy must know the tools of his trade. Among them are secret inks, skeleton keys, fake seals, and a number of deadly devices such as stingers, booby-traps, incendiaries, time-pencils, and gammon grenades. How does he learn to use them? The master spy, or chief organizer, learns their use in a spy school before he goes into the field. But there may be as many as two hundred and fifty men and women in one spy chain, and the master spy entrusts the manual work to his subordinates. He himself does not as a rule pick locks, tamper with packages, or drop a delayed incendiary behind a curtain on a visit to a house during a cocktail party, but it is his job to teach these arts to his followers. It never occurred to me before I went to Pemberley that a spy needs to be a skilful teacher.

To test his teaching ability each candidate had to give a ten-minute demonstration talk on one of these lethal instruments. He knew the subject of his talk two days ahead of time so that he could study the instructions and learn how to handle it. The demonstration talk was also a test of his own familiarity with the equipment and the dexterity and speed with which he could strip and reassemble it.

A candidate who lectured like a professor was hopeless. He had to watch his audience as he went along, making sure they understood each step in the lesson, and letting them handle the instrument themselves. A good candidate would wind up his demonstration talk with, "Now I'm going to show you how to fire this." For the sake of realism the time-pencils and booby-traps held live detonating caps, and the Sten and Bren guns and stingers were loaded with live ammunition. The gammon grenade, however, was so tricky and dangerous that we took out the explosive charge beforehand.

We were always ready to duck behind tables and chairs in case of accidents. The possibility that a candidate might hurt himself or blow a hole through us kept us on the *qui vive*. On a couple of occasions candidates fired Sten rounds into the floor. It was not uncommon for a candidate to get ruffled and trip a booby-trap prematurely or aim the stinger in the general direction of the audience instead of the open window. I believe that some of the candidates enjoyed this assignment very much, because they had us at their mercy. Some of them were old hands with these gadgets and would deliberately fumble at a crucial moment (but actually be well in control of the situation) in order to drive home an important point to the jittery but attentive onlookers. But I don't recall that anyone was ever seriously injured, although there were plenty of close misses and no lack of burned hands. The stinger was a baffling little metal clothes-peg type of gadget, and a man who had not studied it carefully was likely to point it the wrong way round. Before he actually fired the pellet into his belly we would stop him with a quiet "Wait a minute. Are you sure you are holding it right?" Later, in China, I saw a man make the same mistake when he was demonstrating the use of the stinger in a barrack room to a group of his friends. Before I had a chance to warn him, he drilled a .22 hole through his stomach.

10 · You're the Boss

MOST of the group problems at Pemberley were leaderless. We wanted to see who would emerge as leaders and whether the others of the group were willing or recalcitrant followers. But there are some men who are not able to assert leadership in competition with others, and yet can do a first-rate job when the lead is assigned to them. In recognition of this we set up a series of leadership problems in each of which we ourselves designated one candidate as the leader. One of us would take him aside and tell him:

"You have been appointed as the leader in this particular problem. You are the boss, and what you say goes. Now I'll give you your instructions."

Among these "you're the boss" problems were, Find the Secret Message, The Sabotage Plan, The Highest Hill, The Wounded Soldier, and (the two I liked best), Crossing the Border, and The Madman.

The scene of Crossing the Border was a winding road with woods on either side. As we came in sight of the road, walking on a trail through the woods, these instructions were given to the leader:

"You are the leader of a patrol group. You have been in enemy territory. Unfortunately, one of your men has been wounded and must be taken back to your own country across the border. That road is the border, and you can see that this path leads to the road. All six of you must get across without being caught. Here is a stretcher for the wounded man. Put one man in it. Remember, there is a border guard on patrol on that road. He is armed and will shoot to kill if he suspects anyone of trying to cross the border without authority. Don't let him see you. Don't let him hear you. If he should spot you, don't try to overpower him, because you will get hurt. You have twenty minutes. Begin now."

The solution was quite simple. It hinged on the use of the path which led through the woods to the road. The men would come along this path until they were close to the road but still hidden by the trees. As the guard walked to the other end of the road around the bend, one of the men would cross the road and hide in a steep gully on the other side without being seen or heard, if he were cautious. Another man would follow him. Then the two stretcher-bearers would carry the wounded man across the road and climb down the gully with the help of the men already there. The leader would give signals for the crossings and keep a lookout. He was the last to cross. If the men were nimble and alert and worked as a team under the leader's orders they could all make the crossing before the guard came back round the bend.

But if they fell to bickering, or talked too loud, or stepped on twigs, the guard would hear them and come running in their direction, shooting into the woods to drive the fugitives into the open. Naturally he shot blanks at them but they had no way of testing this.

I was surprised that so many of the leaders would try to cross the border without having first spent some time in observing the movements of the guard and the lay of the land. They had only to watch him for a few minutes to realize that when he had rounded the bend in the road he could not see what was going on at the other end. Some leaders tried to make the crossing at the point where the road curved most, halfway from either end of it. Here they could be seen by the guard from either end of the road. Others led their men into the thick of the woods, through tangled undergrowth and dry, crackling boughs. Before they could reach the road the noise of the snapping twigs and scuffed leaves would alert the guard. A few forgot their instructions so far as to jump the guard and attempt to overpower him. The guard was a tough British sergeant, an expert with the butt of his rifle. If they tangled with him they wound up with a bruise on the jaw or a bump on the noggin.

The successful leader would usually begin by saying something like this:

"Now look here, fellows, here's the problem," and he would explain it to them carefully with gestures and by pointing. "First, let's scout the territory. Jack, you go up there and watch the guard. Jim, you watch him from over there. Tom, you look after Harry, who has been wounded, and see he is comfortable while we make plans. Listen, men, let's not have any noise. We have only twenty minutes to get across in. I want to have your advice when you come back from scouting. Don't waste time. Be back here in less than ten minutes, if possible. Let's not talk at all, or if you must talk, whisper into each other's ears. Ed, come with me. We'll take a look at the place where the path joins the road. Eyes and ears open for the guard."

There were some leaders foolish enough to throw stones or pieces of wood in the direction of the guard in the hope that he would go to investigate the missiles and allow the group to cross at another point. Instead, the guard would blow a shrill blast on his whistle, shout madly for reinforcements, and fire at random into the woods to rout out the intruders.

This problem, and also The Madman, could be used to test the snafu tolerance of the leader as well as the subversive talents of one of his followers. In that case I would saunter up alongside the man we had picked for the double-crosser, while we were all walking through the woods to the scene of the problem, and tell him in a low voice that I wanted to talk to him. We would unobtrusively fall behind the others as they straggled along behind their leader and the MTO who was giving him his instructions. When they were all ahead of us so that there was no risk of being overheard, I would say to my man:

"Listen to me carefully. You have an important job to do. Make believe you're co-operating, make believe you're playing fair and square, but manage to bollix up this problem as thoroughly as you can without getting blamed for it. Your job is to prevent the leader from succeeding."

When we had planted a double-crosser on the team it was almost impossible for the leader to succeed in solving the problem. The rotten apple would ask to hear the instructions again; talk too loud and laugh out of place; go off in the wrong direction; slyly belittle the leader's efforts and egg the others on to change the plans or turn the lead over to someone else; encourage the leader to carry out an unworkable scheme if he were stupid enough to propose one; lash the others to a frenzy of impatience by urging all-out haste before the plan had been properly explained. Sometimes the leader would spot the troublemaker, and twice this led to a fist fight.

If the leader insisted to me that one of the team had ruined the problem I might say, "Well, now, look here. I'll drop him out of the next problem, if you like, and give you another chance."

Then, while I gave the leader his instructions for the next problem, another MTO would choose someone else in the group as double-crosser and set the trap again.

We were trying to discover how well the leader could analyze his own mistakes and whether he would try to throw the blame upon another man, rightly or wrongly. Of course, there is not very much a leader can do when a member of his team is secretly working against him. That we recognized. On these occasions we were less interested in the solving of the problem than in the reactions of the leader. He was always a man whose prospective field assignment would call for a great deal of "snafu tolerance," and it was for this reason that we tested him under the strain of a harrowing series of frustrations. The man who abhors chaos and confusion and who cannot endure disappointments had better stay out of the spy business.

The Madman came immediately after Crossing the Border and we gave instructions for it in the same manner. This time I would single out the man we had chosen as leader and walk ahead with him up a gentle, grassy slope to the scene of the problem. If there was to be a doublecrosser the other MTO would meanwhile sidle up to him and slyly coach him in his part. Down below us lay the village, and above us was a stretch of woods. As I briefed the leader I led the way up to a small clearing surrounded by trees on three sides, where I knew the madman was sporting. I told the leader:

"Down there in the village is an insane asylum. We were told this morning that one of the inmates, a violent madman, had escaped with a stolen rifle, with one round in it. You are the leader of the search party scouting the woods, trying to capture this madman. You must catch him. He is very dangerous. See to it that he doesn't shoot any of you. Remember he does have a rifle with one round in it. You have half an hour."

As I spoke we came in sight of the clearing. There was the madman. He had lighted a fire under a big tree and was boiling a kettle on it while he danced around, muttering to himself. The madman was the same talented sergeant who had played the recruit. As soon as I spotted him

I cried, "There he is!" seized the leader by the arm and threw myself on my face, dragging the leader down with me. The madman saw us, let out a piercing yell, and pointed his finger at us as we peered at him over the crest of the hill. We crawled back on our bellies to a clump of bushes on the hillside, out of sight of the madman, where the others were waiting. Only then did I stand up. If the leader stood up before this it was a black mark against him in my book, for the madman could have shot him. Some leaders would ask, "What shall I do?" I would shrug my shoulders and answer, "I've given you the instructions. You're the boss now. Go ahead." It was then up to the leader to assemble his group, explain the problem, and develop a workable plan for catching the madman and getting the gun away from him.

This was the hardest of all the leadership problems. For the leader we always chose a man who had already shown powers of leadership in the earlier problems, to see how he would handle a really tough one. A weak man assigned as leader would have been certain to muff the whole thing. One difficulty was that once the leader had sent out his men in various directions into the woods he could not reassemble them. They were scattered and he must make no noise that might alarm the madman. So the leader had to think out his plan carefully in advance and explain it clearly so that each man in the group understood what to do. Unlike the border guard, the madman was quite unpredictable. When he was caught, it was through luck as much as the leader's skill. The problem was not very often solved, but our main interest lay in the leader's plan of attack and control over his men, and in his analysis of his own tactics after the problem was over. We particularly wanted to know if he could see other possible solutions besides the one he had chosen.

It was easy for a double-crosser to throw a monkey-wrench into the leader's plan without being detected. All he had to do was throw a stone or pieces of wood at the madman to warn him he was being hunted, or encourage another man to speak to the madman. It is a curious thing that in every group there was at least one man who fancied he had a special knack for dealing with a lunatic. "Leave him to me," he would say. "I know how to handle him," and he would disobey the leader's orders and come out into the open to argue or joke with the madman or try to distract his attention. The leader needed plenty of snafu tolerance.

Anyone who tries to use persuasion in dealing with an armed madman is not too sane himself. In many forms of insanity the victim is quite unable to reason coherently, especially if he suffers from delusions or hallucinations. Nevertheless, some leaders did try to reason with the madman. As a rule he readily agreed to come out without his rifle and actually started towards the leader but then, at the last moment, just as the men were ready to pounce on him, he would change his mind, rush back and snatch up his gun and point it at anyone who approached him, all the while cackling with demented laughter and shouting, "Come a bit nearer so I won't miss!" If the search party retreated he would go back to his fire under the tree, prop his gun against a stump, rub his hands together and warm them at the flames, brew himself tea, whistle, burst into snatches of song, mumble to himself, chuckle at his own jokes, and now and then scream like a Canadian loon. His behavior was never the same twice running but it was always crazy. From time to time he would leave his fire to stroke and fondle his gun or peer into the woods.

The best leaders usually left the madman by his stump and his fire until the men had surrounded him on the woods on three sides. The gun was the key to the problem. Sometimes two men would jump him at once, one bringing him down with a tackle while the other snatched his gun away, but this was risky. Or, when the gun was leaning against the tree-stump, one man would rush the madman while the other man got between him and the gun. The madman was always careful to give a number of opportunities for them to take his gun away, but if they hesitated, back he would be at the stump, patting and stroking the rifle. In some groups there were men who could give signals by imitating bird-calls, but, so as not to attract the interest of the madman, they had to be bird-calls of the English countryside. Sometimes the men were around him, hiding behind trees, just about to make the rush—when he would hear a noise, yell, "they are after me," grab his rifle and walk out on the open side of the clearing. To us it was a sign that the half-hour was up. As the round-shouldered madman walked down the clearing and into the road, holding his rifle by the barrel and letting the stock of it bump along the ground behind him, it meant to the group that they had (like so many other groups before them) failed the problem.

11 · Red Is Blue and Up Is Down

MY FATHER had a dog called Leo, half English setter and half cocker spaniel. During the pheasant season when Leo was told to "go and get it" he would pick up the scent and follow it through till he came upon the bird, then freeze into a point, nose ahead, tail straight out behind, till we flushed out the bird. Modern psychologists would call Leo "goal-oriented." He was not distracted by frisky mongrels or untrained whelps working the same field, nor even by the smell of rabbit. Had he been able to read, Leo could have outshone many of the candidates in the problem I am going to describe next. Unlike Leo, many of them became muddled and forgot their instructions in the problem we called "Red is Blue and Up is Down."

The candidates were lined up side by side and about three feet apart in one of the rooms of the house. I told them, "Until I give you permission you are henceforth not to speak to anyone except me. This is a strict rule. If you violate it, you will automatically be failed in this problem and dropped without being allowed to complete it. And even when you speak to me, do not speak aloud but come to see me yourself. It is very important to follow your instructions exactly. I will now pass out to each of you instructions which you must read and memorize. When you are absolutely sure that you know them, nod to me and I will pick up your card."

I then passed out a card to each man. The men were too far apart to read each other's cards. The first man's card read: "You are to go through an obstacle course. The instructions you must follow are: When you come to an obstacle marked with a red sign, go to the left of it; if it is marked with a blue sign, go to the right of it. If it has an 'A' mark on it, go over it. If it has a 'B' mark on it, go under it. *These are your only instructions. There are no other instructions. Follow them precisely.*"

The second man in the line did not have these instructions. His were just the opposite: Go to the right of the red, left of the blue, under the "A" and over the "B." Men Nos. 3 and 5 would have the same instructions as No. 1, and Nos. 4 and 6 the same instructions as No. 2, etc. A candidate who tried to follow the fellow in front or watch the man behind would make mistakes. In this test, suggestibility was a serious handicap.

After they had memorized their instructions, I picked up the cards, again cautioned the men against any talking whatsoever, even to themselves out loud, and led them in single file out onto a grassy lawn terrace which had a flight of steps leading down to the obstacle course. The course consisted of benches, small bridges, underground passages, a stepladder, crotches of trees, ropes between trees, a tent, a children's swing, ropes suspended from trees, pools of water, and a variety of vertical and horizontal log bar barriers. Most of the obstacles had either a red, blue, "A" or "B" mark on them, but to make things a bit more confusing, some of them were not marked at all. Some had arrows pointing to the left or right, suggesting that the candidate should go in that direction. All the obstacles were numbered. The first obstacle was marked 1, the second 2, the third 3, but after that it became a potpourri. If the candidate took the arrows or the numbers into account he would get thoroughly muddled, and if he tried to take both arrows and numbers into account, he would get lost in the middle of the course. And to make sure that there was a plethora of distracting stimuli, a sergeant was waiting for us at the bottom of the steps. The candidates knew him as one of the waiters: mild-mannered, warm-hearted, courteous and co-operative, the last man in the world to do you a dirty trick. As I finished lining up the men, one behind another, three feet apart, each with a clear view of the sergeant and the entire course, I said, "Okay, Sergeant, go ahead. Run the course." "Thank you, sir," he answered and took off walking briskly yet cautiously, just as they had often seen him walking with trays of dishes to the dining-room. As the candidates fastened eager eyes upon him I said to them, "If you wish, you may watch the sergeant as he runs the course. As soon as he has completed the second obstacle, student No. 1 will go ahead, and as soon as No. 1 has completed the second obstacle No. 2 will go ahead, and so on. Please do not waste time."

When the sergeant came to the first obstacle, a rope strung four feet high between two poles, with a "B" marker, he tried to leap over it. This was right for Nos. 2, 4, and 6 but wrong for Nos. 1, 3, and 5. As he jumped, he tripped over the rope and almost fell but quickly regained his balance, in a way that made the candidates feel sorry for him rather than inclined to laugh. He tightened the rope again carefully, and went on to the second obstacle, which was correctly numbered. It was interesting to watch the men as he tried to jump the rope. Candidates 2, 4, and 6 would nod their heads to themselves in approval and sometimes smile knowingly. But candidates 1, 3, and 5 would scratch their heads or rub their chins or hunch their shoulders, and peer even more intently at the sergeant, as though they were not quite sure of what they had just seen. Coming to the second obstacle, the sergeant noted the red marker and went to the left of it, which pleased Nos. 1, 3, and 5 but puzzled Nos. 2, 4, and 6. No. 1 had to start out now.

Though he had been instructed to go under obstacles marked "B," he usually followed the sergeant, tried to jump the rope and fell flat on his face, raising a laugh from the others. Then when No. 2 started he would do the same thing, because his instructions were that he should go over obstacles marked "B"—as both the sergeant and No. 1 had done. No. 2 would usually decide to follow No. 1 or the sergeant throughout the course.

Meanwhile the sergeant had gone to the left of the second obstacle, the bench, and run completely around it, following the arrows. Then he scratched his head, stepped on the bench, and walked from one end to the other. This bit of irrelevancy confused No. 1, at least. He had to ponder the solution, which no longer seemed to be a simple one. It also confused the men still on the line waiting to run the course. As the sergeant proceeded, it always appeared that he was "reasoning" his way along, sometimes hesitantly, sometimes with a big, broad grin as he completed an obstacle and looked back at it proudly, as if to say, no, sir, he wasn't afraid to go under log tunnels, filled with mucky clay, and walk in and out of water-filled trenches, even when these obstacles were not marked at all.

Each candidate running this course was observed by one professional staff member at Pemberley, and every single move the candidate made was traced on a map of the course, just as a psychologist traces the path of a white rat in a maze. At the end of the course, each observer took his candidate aside and asked him what rules he had followed, and why he did thus and so at particular obstacles, to see how he would rationalize his own actions. The candidate often had a shock when he was shown the card of instructions that he had been given before he began the course and asked to explain why he had not followed them.

The test itself was childishly simple. There were only two rules to remember, and when these rules were followed, there were no difficult physical obstacles or hazards. Socks would be dry, breath left to spare, tempers unfrayed, and clothes untorn. All candidates had been told to follow their instructions exactly, once by me orally and twice on their cards. Yet in spite of this many were easily deceived by watching the man in front or the man behind or the tomfoolery of the sergeant or by the arrows, numbers, and unmarked obstacles.

Why did they make so many mistakes in this particular problem? There are, of course, scores of different reasons. But it seems to me that the main source of error in all cases arose from the fact that we are social animals. We depend upon the ideas of others around us. When there is someone in the group who has prestige and status, or whom we believe to have more brains than we have, then we naturally assume that he must be right, that he cannot be wrong, and so we do as he does. Time and again candidates failed this problem who had obtained superior ratings on problems where there were no conflicting instructions or misleading clues. We were, of course, on the lookout for the sheep as well as for the man who could maintain his own orientation and follow his own goals, in spite of a host of distracting stimuli. By the time we came to run this problem we had already learned quite a bit about the candidates, because it was the last on the four-day program.

Those of us who worked intimately with the candidates on outside problems developed a strange ability to call the shots on their success in this problem. Just how we did it is a mystery to me now as it was a mystery to me then. The combination of qualities we looked for was never the same. Sometimes the successful candidate was highly gregarious, at other times unsociable; sometimes very intelligent, and at other times narrow-minded and rigid. We were never able to define the combination of qualities that made for outstanding success or abject failure. But our staff, men who had all had field experience, believed that it was of great value to know a man's showing on this test before sending him into the field. Of the well-screened, generally high-calibre candidates who came to Pemberley, about one in ten was able to go straight through the course without a single error, and one or two out of ten were bound to bollix themselves up so completely we had to rescue them from themselves at the end of the half-hour.

I would like to see experimental psychologists carry out studies to analyze and factor out the mental and emotional attributes involved in such a problem and to show their relationships to different occupations and life problems.

I remember a strange performance on this test. Willy was a reformed *roué*, about thirty years old, American by birth, who had lived in Paris most of his life. His father was a millionaire, Willy was a millionaire, thanks to a grandfather who had done all the work. Besides drinking and whoring, he spent most of his civilian life trying both legally and illegally to get hold of his father's money, while his father was trying to get hold of Willy's money. Willy went through the obstacle course without making a single mistake. It was a perfect performance. When I approached him for the interview, he asked, before I had a chance to say a word, "May I go through the course once more? I know I can do better." "Of course," I replied. This time he went *completely* wrong. Fore was aft and hind was front. He reported back within a few minutes grinning proudly. When I asked him why he did things so differently this time, he said, with a straight face, "The first time I followed the instructions which I was given, but they did not tally with what the others were doing, and so I knew I must be wrong. So I've gone through it again, doing just the reverse. I think now I've done it right."

To this day, I haven't been able to find out what makes Willy tick, but I suspect that on that particular problem he was pulling my leg.

12 · Elbows on the Table

PEOPLE who know they are under observation are going to wear party manners. We wanted to find out how the candidates behaved with their shirt sleeves rolled up and their elbows on the table. It may not seem like fair play, but while the candidates were at Pemberley they might just as well have been under the eyes of the Russian secret police. They were constantly under surveillance, sometimes even with field-glasses. How can you learn to know a man inside out unless you keep watching him, especially when he is off guard?

An MTO at Pemberley had to have a split personality. While we ran the problems we were objective and noncommittal. We would not even spare a smile or a frown unless it was called for as part of the test. But when we joined the candidates for lunch we tried to create an atmosphere of sporting camaraderie. We would chat gaily in the group's native language—if we spoke it—and raise all sorts of topics for discussion. This honeyed treatment caught a fair proportion of flies.

On one occasion I induced a group of Frenchmen at my

table to discuss psychology. They had no inkling that I was a psychologist. In the course of the conversation one of the men tried to explain the theories of Adler, the Viennese psychologist who popularized the inferiority complex. This candidate was soon out of his depth, but one of his companions broke into the talk and explained with great clarity the concepts of Adler, Jung, and Freud, and the differences between scientific psychology and the clinical concepts of the psychoanalysts. Everybody was impressed. I thanked him for his explanation and as I was about to leave I said, "You must be a psychologist." He reddened, but smiled politely and replied, "Oh, non, mon lieutenant, je ne suis pas. Merci." I knew he was lying. Months later I met him again, this time behind the lines in France, and found out that I had called the shot correctly.

The less naïve among the candidates knew that however friendly we seemed at the lunch table we were at heart the same hard-boiled, cold-blooded observers who had put them through situation tests. Often they engaged in verbal fencing with us. They would pay us compliments, toss our questions back at us, pry information from us which we were reluctant to give.

They resented our implied superiority. A candidate might be a colonel or a brigadier, a knight or a duke, a distinguished author or a multi-millionaire, but we treated them all just as we treated the enlisted men and noncoms on the Pemberley staff. These enlisted men, "other ranks" as the British call them, were treated civilly, but not as friends. If they were inefficient they were spoken to sharply. That's the custom. That's the army. Let 'em grumble. Grumble they did, but in general terms. *This brought them very, very close to the candidates who also wanted to grumble, generally and specifically, or just talk about themselves.* Their grudges, hopes, fears, ambitions were revealed not to the officers but to the enlisted men, these poor, miserable unfortunate fellow creatures who, unlike the candidates themselves, had to remain at Pemberley and continue to suffer indignities!

There was a bar at Pemberley for the candidates and enlisted men, but we officers had our drinks served in the officers' mess. In the bar the candidates grew friendly with the enlisted men, stood them beers, and now and then Scotches, and sometimes at the end of the four-day program treated them to a hilarious drinking spree. Real names, past experiences, whole life-histories were kicked around. Security was forgotten.

Those candidates who failed may not have suspected it then, but they may as well learn it now as they read these pages. *Every one* of those privates, corporals, and sergeants had been trained as observers in the assessment program for spy selection. At least three-fourths of them had fought in the Battle of France and escaped at Dunkirk. Some had been on intelligence missions. All who had been in action had been wounded, some severely. They did not think that war was a laughing matter for careless fools. About half of them were, in addition, trained professional psychologists or psychological assistants, with B.A. or M.A. degrees from Oxford, Cambridge, London or Edinburgh. Their reports on each candidate, what he said and did, to whom, where, when and how, were submitted in writing to those of us on the "inside" staff.

Guy was one man whom we rejected largely on the basis of these reports. He was an American, a professional army man, brave, loyal, patriotic, the finest West Point type. We were assessing him for work in France. He spoke French perfectly and was familiar with the area to which he would be sent. But he was too conspicuous. A spy must not be conspicuous, and I don't just mean he must not have six fingers. Guy was tall and handsome, with the proud bearing of an aristocrat. He would not tolerate the slightest criticism. If he were not treated like a nobleman he would bristle and want to fight. In spite of his assets, we turned him down.

Now, it was usually to a man's own advantage to accept the findings of the Assessment Board with a good grace. These findings, even if they punctured his ego, might save his life. But Guy was outraged. His sponsoring officials appealed his case to the colonel in charge of all British selection and training, and won their appeal. Guy was dropped behind the lines in Northern France and began his work as a resistance organizer.

On one of his trips with a number of his men he was stopped by the Gestapo for a routine check-up. The Frenchmen, accustomed to these routine inspections and fearful of the Germans, were cowed and subservient, but Guy was haughty and dignified, implying that the Germans were nothing but inferior coolies. They checked his papers and those of his men and drove on, but after going about half a mile they changed their minds, turned around, came back and picked up Guy and his men who were still trying to start the gazogene engine of their car. Guy was grilled and tortured by the Gestapo. He never broke down, never gave himself or his friends away. The Germans finally decided his story must be true. Guy lived to be set free at the end of the war, but he was so badly injured that he had to give up his cherished career in the army and is today a disappointed and embittered man.

Most of the candidates enjoyed taking the situation tests. It was like going back to their childhood to play cops and robbers. They looked forward with less pleasure to their interrogation by a psychiatrist, testing by a psychologist, and interview with the Commanding Officer, which were also part of the four-day assessment.

When I came to Pemberley one of the staff psychiatrists was a Viennese refugee, a thin, intense man with a great flow of words. He spent his spare time in writing a book on the Rorschach (ink-blot) Test and in hunting gray squirrels. The woods on the estate were full of them. He would shoot them through the head with a .22 rifle, skin them, treat the pelts, and save them to make a fur coat for his wife. He was an astute judge of men and was especially skilful in detecting little tricks of speech and manner which distinguish Germans from Austrians and Jews from non-Jews. His verdict, "This man cannot pass for long as a Nazi German," saved the life of many a courageous Jewish or Austrian candidate. I liked and admired the squirrel-hunter, and I hope his book on the Rorschach has sold well.

The staff at Pemberley was constantly changing. The Squirrel-hunter was replaced by a psychiatrist known as Fred. He was proud of his nickname, but it suited him as ill as the major's uniform he wore. Fred was Egyptian by birth, gentle, kind and sympathetic, apt to judge candidates by their hopes and ambitions rather than by their actual capacities. During an interview he would keep gently stroking his briefcase on the desk. He hated to fail a candidate, even the most inept.

While the psychiatrists delved into the emotions the psychologists were concerned mainly with intellectual factors. (This dualism is unfortunately characteristic of British psychiatry and psychology.) The psychological tests included:

(a) *A verbal intelligence test in the candidate's native language.*

(b) *A non-verbal intelligence test, primarily for illiterates.*

(c) *A code-aptitude test.* The code-aptitude test was given to all candidates, but those who were being considered as radio operators were required to earn a higher score. All spies trained in Britain had to learn to send and receive radio messages in Morse code. The British made a point of this. Even though a spy usually took a trained radio operator with him on a mission, he himself must be able to send and receive not less than ten words a minute. Then if his radio operator were ill, injured or killed (the death-rate among radio operators in the field is high), the spy could at least ask London to send him another, fingering out his message at the slow rate of eight or ten words per minute. In these days of rapid communication, anyone who plans to make a career of espionage would be wise to take a course or two in radio sending and receiving.

(d) *Mechanical aptitude and proficiency tests.* Was the candidate skilful with his hands? A spy may have to set booby-traps in the dark, repair his radio, clean and adjust his weapons, and in many other ways think with his fingers.

(e) *Tests of temperament and personality such as the Rorschach and Thematic Apperception.*

(f) *Buddy ratings.* After three days at Pemberley the candidates in a group were asked to rank, rate, and describe themselves and the others in the group in terms of many different traits. One of the questions was: Which of your associates would you prefer to have as (1) Leader, (2) Subordinate, (3) Number Two Man? In each case, give the reasons for your choice.

The psychologists used the same rating system as the MTO's. On the wall of the officers' dining-room we set up a rating panel which we called the Big Board. Under the heading of each situation problem or paper-and-pencil test was a row of nails, and on each nail we hung a colored poker chip with a hole in it. Each rating had a different color. Inspection of a candidate's line on the Big Board revealed the general trend of his performance. One man might do well on individual problems but poorly on those involving relations with others. Another might do well on paper-and-pencil tests but poorly on situation tests. There were many different sorts of possible combinations of aptitudes and proficiencies. We always studied the Big Board carefully before writing our own final report.

A candidate's interview with the Commanding Officer might last one hour or it might last four hours. The Commanding Officer at this point knew nothing of the candidate's performance on tests or of his psychiatric interview, but judged him simply as a man he might or might not want to have with him in the field. There were three successive Commanding Officers during my stay at Pemberley, all of them men of shrewd mind and strong character. The first, Colonel Carey, was a steel-mill owner, a tough old man, but absolutely fair, neither more nor less kind to the dull than to the bright. He might spend hours talking with a candidate, but once he had come to a decision, that was it. No more time to waste. I looked on him as the epitome of British justice.

One Saturday Colonel Carey left. There was no prior announcement, no shaking of hands or goodbyes. On Monday the Adjutant told us that Colonel Smythe, the second in command, was now our boss. Smythe, a schoolmaster, was inclined to stress brains. Force of character without intelligence he regarded as a drawback. When Smythe was away his place was taken by his deputy, Major Montague of the Grenadier Guards. Montague, a Scot, was one of the most charming men I have ever met. He had a weakness for the type of candidate who was, as he put it, "a decent chap," whether or not he happened to be suited for espionage.

All three Commanding Officers, Carey, Smythe, and

Montague, would flatly reject a candidate whose honesty was even in question. As they explained to me, a spy, by the very nature of his job, works largely without supervision. Huge sums of money are turned over to him to carry out his mission and he has a great deal of latitude in the way he disposes of them. Hundreds of thousands of dollars may be washed down the drain on one single dishonest spy. If he is clever as well as crooked, he can become rich at the expense of the nation that backs him with the rights of citizenship and trusts him with its secrets.

One candidate, an American major, had been a professional gambler before the war. He had a splendid record at Pemberley, but Smythe failed him without a qualm, saying, "I cannot understand how the United States Army ever commissioned a man who has been a gambler. I for one refuse to approve this man's going into the field as leader of an intelligence team." The candidate openly admitted that when he had a pair of dice in his hands his ethics were shaky, but insisted that when in the service of his country he was hard-working and loyal. When the gambler found he could not go on an intelligence mission he joined an infantry battalion which hit the Normandy beaches on D-Day. The colonel in charge was seriously wounded and Old Pro, the gambling major, took charge. He coolly regrouped the battalion, and led them back into the thick of the fight, pushing back a German onslaught which had threatened to rip the Allied lines in two. He was awarded the Distinguished Service Cross. Was Smythe unduly harsh in rejecting him? We shall never know.

I am sure he made a mistake in the case of another American officer. Smythe asked this young Lieutenant, "Why did you become an O.S.S. paratrooper?"

"I don't know," he answered, shrugging his shoulders. "Maybe it was because my pal Joe did it, and I do what Joe does. I have a lot of confidence in Joe, and, of course, Colonel, we get a hundred bucks a month extra in the paratroops."

Smythe was shocked. He wasn't used to men who were so forthright about their own motives. He had expected the lieutenant to say something about wanting to serve his country and take an active part in the war. Most candidates gave this sort of answer, more because they thought it the proper thing to say than because they had actually examined their own motives. Smythe failed the lieutenant as a field saboteur on the grounds of "poor motivation." Later he became an instructor in an intelligence training school in Scotland. He did well, and managed to be sent on several O.S.S. missions into Norway and Denmark, along with his pal, Joe. They both distinguished themselves in the field, and then volunteered to work for O.S.S. in China.

Smythe was on sure ground when it came to picking Englishmen, and I learned a great deal from him. He chose men who were tough without showing it. One of these was Alex, a Cambridge graduate, a small, slender young man with a swarthy skin and a shock of black hair. He claimed to be Scotch but he looked more like a Latin. He had lived so long abroad, particularly in France, that he even spoke English with a slight French accent. Alex had knocked around. He had been a jockey. (Once he had been barred from the turf for obscure reasons, but he did not tell this to Smythe.) He fought with the International Brigade in Spain as a lieutenant. Then he changed sides and fought with Franco to get a promotion to captain. When he came to Pemberley he had just completed twenty-four Commando raids on the enemy coast. His unimpressive looks and soft, deprecating manner hid a fierce fighting spirit. Smythe picked him for a resistance organizer in France.

Alex was dropped into Central France in February, 1944. He bought a bicycle and went about his business of organizing resistance in his area. Day after day he pumped his bicycle uphill and downhill, over highways and dirt roads, as calmly as a mailman making his rounds. Once or twice he was frisked by the Nazis but they did not molest him. He looked like a million other Frenchmen. When his net was tight, Alex and his men went into action. The Germans were shot at wherever they travelled. On one occasion Alex and two of his men wiped out thirty-four of the enemy with grenades and Sten guns. At last the Germans stayed huddled in their garrison cities and refused to police the roads any more. When Alex finished with France, he went to Burma. For all I know, he may be there yet.

13 · Taping the Candidates

ON THE last afternoon of a group's stay at Pemberley there was always a staff conference. We assembled at four o'clock in the officers' dining-room, which was also our conference room, to read and listen to reports on the candidates and reach a final decision about each one. The Commanding Officer presided at the head of the table, with the psychologists and psychiatrists on his left and the MTO's on his right. Conducting Officers, and visitors from London headquarters who were interested in the fate of particular candidates, sat at the far end of the table.

My report was always in terms of the job for which the candidate was being assessed, whether that of radio operator, resistance organizer, intelligence chief, courier, cut-out, field instructor or saboteur. I would describe the job in detail, point out the candidate's assets and shortcomings for that job, and then make my recommendations. There were three reports read on each candidate, one by an MTO, one by a psychiatrist which included the findings of the psychologist, and one by the Commanding Officer. Each report ended by rating the candidate in terms of the job on a scale from A to E. A single E rating meant that the candidate would be failed, regardless of how high his other two ratings might be.

The MTO reports seldom took longer than ten minutes to read, but the psychiatric-psychological report often took half an hour. There was some good-natured rivalry between us, and we MTO's insisted that the length of the report was in inverse ratio to the amount of time spent in collecting the data.

Sometimes we disagreed. I reported that one candidate was not very brave while Fred described him as a man of courage. I meant that he had belly-crawled the high plank instead of walking it, and had refused to jump from the platform to the rope or attempt to swing across the barb wire. Fred meant that he had worked his way through college and then started a law practice in a strange town and made a go of it. The MTO's took a cross-sectional view, asking "What is the man now?" without trying to discover how he became so. The psychiatrists and psychologists took a longitudinal, life-history view. Both points of view are needed to form a clear picture of a personality.

The Commanding Officer gave his report last. It took only about five minutes and dealt with the qualities the candidate had revealed in the interview. After the reports had been read we would discuss the candidate and agree upon a final rating. If we could not agree, the lowest rating would be accepted as the official one. Then the Commanding Officer would turn to the Conducting Officers and the visitors and ask, "Do you think we have reached a fair decision?" If they felt we had been unfair they could appeal our decision by writing to the Brigadier in charge of Selection and Training.

There was one officer from American Headquarters who often appealed our decisions. He had himself been turned down as a resistance organizer. He was especially likely to appeal if the candidate came from his own State, Louisiana. One of his hot-blooded Creoles made himself a nuisance at Pemberley. He had scarcely arrived there before he began making eyes at a beautiful Egyptian girl in his group. He persuaded her to take a walk in the woods with him, but she soon came flying back, breathless, disheveled, and frightened. Later he lost his temper with another candidate, lifted him over his head and threw him into the fireplace. Luckily the screen saved the man from injury. On an outside problem he started a fight with a young man, knocked him down, and refused to let his victim stand up until he had offered an abject apology. We felt so strongly about him that we even hoped he would be dismissed from the American Army, in which he was a captain. Over our vigorous protests he was sent into the field as assistant to a resistance organizer. Within two weeks he refused to obey the order of his French chief to blow up a bridge, and challenged him to a duel with .45 pistols. He was flown out of France in a hurry to face court-martial charges in London.

The Chief Instructor at the Arisaig Paramilitary School in Scotland later told me that, before the Pemberley assessment program was set up, five out of ten students would fail in their training courses. But after Pemberley was in operation and the rule established that candidates had to pass Pemberley before going on to training, only one out of ten failed the course at Arisaig. One of the ten percent who failed was a New York manufacturer who had started his own business and was making more than $75,000 a year. O.S.S. recruited him to organize resistance in France, because he had lived there for many years and had many business contacts there. He was devoted to his family, wrote to his wife every day, and counted the day lost when he did not hear from her. At Pemberley he was lonely and despondent, always talking about his wife and children and how much they meant to him. We failed him because we felt that, in spite of his success in business, he had too little self-sufficiency and lone-wolfishness to be a resistance organizer. The sponsoring officials at the final conference disagreed with us, and arranged for him to go to the Arisaig School for four weeks pending an appeal of his case.

At Arisaig he was not allowed to send or receive letters. The rule was enforced in order to accustom the men to the isolation they would find in the field. At the end of the two weeks without letters from his wife this man was a nervous wreck, depressed and incoherent. He recovered after several weeks in the psychiatric ward of an army hospital, but there was no more talk of sending him to France.

Of the candidates who were passed at Pemberley and sent into the field, four out of five were decorated or officially cited for outstanding work. Just the reverse was true of those who were failed at Pemberley but later sent into the field at the request of their sponsoring officials. Four out of five of these were reprimanded, recalled to London, cited for negligence of duty, or court-martialled. And, mind you, these were the cream of the rejected cases. Only when a sponsoring official was quite certain that we were wrong would he have the courage to put his name to a formal request for exemption.

In looking back on the work carried out by the assessment staff at Pemberley, I am struck by one serious limitation. British universities have not so far stressed psychology. To them it is still an adjunct of philosophy. A person who in Britain is called a psychologist does not have the breadth of training and variety of experience of an American psychologist. In consequence the British assessment boards were influenced to a much greater extent by the psychiatrists. In selection work the psychiatrist is handicapped by his training, which has taught him to think first of abnormality. Inexperienced in problems of normal human beings, he is too prone to discover "neurotic traits" and "psychopathic behavior" in every twitch of a muscle. Moreover, the psychiatrist tends to look at assessment from the point of view of the candidate rather than of his prospective employer. He asks himself, "Will rejection be a great blow to this man?" "For his own good, should he not be given this chance?" On the other hand, a psychologist would ask, "Has this man the qualities we are looking for?" "Will he succeed in the jobs we have in mind?" "Will he be an asset to our organization?"

The psychiatrists at Pemberley tended toward leniency, and owing to their dominance over the psychologists some candidates were passed who were not really up to standard. This tendency was counteracted to some extent by the tough-minded and experienced MTO's, but I believe that with better-qualified psychologists the Pemberley Assessment Board would have done an even better job.

14 · The Road to the Isles

MY LIFE at Pemberley was strenuous and stimulating but as months passed by I grew more and more eager to make a reality out of the bluff I had entered on in Washington. I kept comparing myself with the candidates I tested. Most of them had been born abroad or had lived abroad for many years. Each was familiar with the actual area to which he would go and the language he would use there. As a rule it was the tongue he knew best, the tongue in which he thought and dreamed. I had never lived outside the United States but I had other assets. Years of training psychology had taught me not to accept things at their face value, so that I was less naïve than most of the candidates. Also I had listened constantly to the talk of men who had been behind the lines and had learned to think of myself as a hunted man. A spy who forgets that he is a hunted man is not likely to live very long.

France was the only country to which I had any chance of going. Whenever French candidates came to Pemberley I contrived to be one of the MTO's assigned to their group. I gave them instructions, listened to their explanations, answered their questions and chatted with them around the lunch table, all in French. Every day I listened to "Ici Londres," the radio broadcast sent out for General de Gaulle's Free French. Ned Ashley, the Adjutant at Pemberley, was teaching himself French as a hobby. We would listen together to his French language records and criticize one another's efforts to imitate the accent. Sometimes we were brash enough to talk French in front of certain staff members who knew the language well. Their sensitive ears were offended by our gross mistakes in grammar and pronunciation, and they would correct us in exasperated tones.

My plans for going to France were not well received by the Pemberley staff, who suggested most politely that I was putting opium in my tobacco. Smythe, in particular, swore he would never recommend me for an espionage assignment. He regarded it as an unpleasant way for me to commit suicide. Thinking that I was dissatisfied with Pemberley, he went out of his way to be kind. He played two-handed pinochle and gin rummy with me. He recommended me for promotion to first lieutenant. He took me to drink in ancient pubs with picturesque names like "The Bear and Ragged Staff" and "The Goat and Compasses." To steer my mind away from France he asked me to go with him to India, where he was to set up a Selection Assessment Board like Pemberley for the South-East Asia Command, and promised that if I accepted he would have me jumped from first lieutenant to major. I realized I would not succeed with old Smythe by the direct approach.

So I sneaked in the remark one day that I felt inadequately prepared for the work I was doing. Besides his field experience every other MTO had been through all the British intelligence schools. To keep me happy Smythe sent me for a one-week tour in the Highlands of Scotland.

Everyone in England knew that something mysterious was going on in the Northwest Highlands, that hilly, rain-soaked chunk of Scotland cut off from the rest by the Caledonian Canal, a chain of lochs joined together. In peacetime swarms of tourists, English and American, migrate there in summer to fish for salmon in the hill streams, shoot grouse and stalk deer on the heather-covered moors, or merely admire the poetic landscape, but during the war no one was allowed across the Canal without a pass. The Highlands then were a Boy Scout's dream, full of Commando, intelligence and sabotage schools with here and there a camp for untrustworthy aliens.

The Highland crofters and fishermen were undisturbed —more fortunate than those inhabitants of the South Devon coast whose homes were smashed to rubble in the pre-invasion exercises. Most of the young Highlanders went off to fight, but the rest of the family carried on the work of the farm. Owing to the scarcity of labor and transport the local herrings, eggs, and mutton could not be sent to the London markets, so the Commandos, saboteurs, and untrustworthy aliens lived very well indeed in the Highlands. Thirty cents would buy a drink of the finest Scotch whisky.

Before a train crossed the Caledonian Canal every passenger's credentials were searchingly scrutinized by security agents, Scotland Yard detectives, and military police. The only persons allowed across were local residents, staff and students of the training schools, and subversive agents who had been caught working for the enemy. These subversives were "retained in a holding area," or in other words kept safely out of the way. Some were handcuffed and guarded. Others did not even know they had been spotted, but crossed the Canal under the joyful delusion that they were to undergo an intensive training course to prepare them for an important mission. At the training schools they would find the standards unexpectedly high. When they had learned to transmit sixteen words a minute on the radio they would be told to increase their speed to twenty-five words—"it will be a very delicate mission, you know." And so their training would stretch out and out, while the war went on without them. Among these were a number of high-ranking French officers who professed loyalty to the Allied cause but were really working for the Germans. At General de Gaulle's request they were billeted in Northwest Scotland where they could do no more harm.

Once across the Canal I felt like the traveller in "The Road to the Isles." I journeyed to remote places with ancient Celtic names—Arisaig, Mallaig, Garramor, Loch Morar, Meable, Glennacadoch. There I learned about demolitions, map-reading, compass-work, rapid firing, silent killing, fieldcraft, rope-work, tumbling, living off the land, and a few para-naval tactics. The students had to climb hand over hand up precipitous cliffs, swing off high ledges by ropes tied to trees, shoot at moving targets while running over bogs, sand, or rocks, toss live grenades and shoot tracer bullets, hold an advanced post in an empty house against "enemy" fire and deal with an ambush on a lonely road. The problems were as difficult, and some of them almost as dangerous, as anything a man would be likely to face in the field. Ribs were broken, ankles sprained, flesh torn, even limbs lost. A handsome English actor, known all over the world for his brilliant screen performances, was an instructor at one of the schools. In tossing a fragmentation grenade it was the rule, after the release pin was pulled and the grenade activated, to count "one-hundred-and-one, one-hundred-and-two," and then toss it, so as to leave only two seconds before the explosion. This insured that the grenade would explode on the target and not be hurled back at the thrower by an alert foe. One day as he was demonstrating grenade-throwing he counted "one-hundred-and-one, one-hundred-and . . ." when the grenade exploded in his hand, taking his arm off at the elbow. When he came back from the hospital he resumed grenade instruction, tossing the pineapples with his left hand.

The first time I faced the cliff-and-ladder exercise my knees shook. In front of me rose a sheer rock-face two hundred feet high which I had to ascend by a perpendicular iron ladder. The ground was strewn with rocks and boulders and a fall from the ladder meant certain death from a broken neck or a smashed skull. The two hearty young American instructors who were leading us shouted, "Come on, folks," and began clambering up the narrow ladder with the playful agility of gibbons. The students followed, trying dutifully to look enthusiastic under the watchful eyes of the two British instructors who were last in line. The student in front of me took one look at the ladder, blenched, and turned away muttering, "This is not for me." No one paid any attention, but the British instructors called out cheerily, "Let's go, men, let's go. We don't have much time before dinner."

I glanced up once more at the dizzy height—dizzy to me, but I suppose it would be nothing to a fireman—set my teeth and started the upward climb, saying to myself, "If they can do it, so can I." As usual it was a rainy day and the rungs of the ladder were slippery with slime, but I soon learned the trick of hooking one foot and one arm behind the rungs to steady myself while I pulled up. Nearing the top and pleased with my progress I made the mistake of looking down. The sight of the jagged rocks below turned me giddy. But the instructors were always on the lookout for signs of "freezing," and a jovial shout of "Let's get a move on, men. Who's holding up the parade?" snapped me out of my momentary fright. Soon I was at the top.

From the top of the cliff a rope and pulley ran down at an angle to the ground, like the device for transporting skiers up steep slopes. Here, however, I had to travel down, not up, and instead of a ski-basket there was only a wooden bar. Grasping the bar with both hands I stepped off the cliff-top into the air, and shot down along the rope at terrific speed. Large heaps of sand had thoughtfully been strewn at the far end of the rope where I landed with a thud.

Next day the instructors put us through it again, and the next day, and the next. By the time I had negotiated the ladder and rope six days running I realized that the danger was not so great as it looked. For a weakling or a man in poor condition, yes, it would be hazardous, but these had been weeded out already. Every student, man or woman, who came to the Scottish training schools was strong and nimble and in the pink of condition. The rope-and-ladder exercise was to test nerve, not muscle. No student ever fell from the ladder or off the cliff, but several balked. Some didn't feel too well today; maybe they'd do it tomorrow. Others, like the man before me, flatly refused to try.

The Headquarters of the Scottish Schools was at Arisaig. It was the Chief Instructor at Arisaig who told me that before Pemberley was set up to screen candidates, five out of ten men dinged out of training, but now only one out of ten could not make the grade. The instructors were grateful to us, because now they could spend their time training students rather than writing letters to London asking that dunderheads be dropped from the course. All the same they could not resist pulling the legs of visiting members of the Pemberley staff.

The Chief Medical Officer at Arisaig, Captain Mackenzie, told me about a recent visit of Major Beaufort, one of the Pemberley psychiatrists. This Beaufort was a brilliant man, bursting with ideas, many of them sound and practical, but he was vain and self-satisfied and always telling people how clever he was. After a while even Beaufort's friends would tire of his constant demands for more and more ego juice.

He made the trip to Arisaig to check on the progress of some of the candidates he had selected for training. The staff of the Arisaig school was properly notified in advance so that it would accord Major Beaufort the trappings and ceremonies which he felt were his due. The staff did itself proud. Major Beaufort was met at the station by a shining Morris driven by one of the best British Army chauffeurs, punctilious in his salutes and courtesies. In the Officers' Mess, all the staff were awaiting him. Major Beaufort was delighted, and graciously joined in the small talk at the tea table. Toward the end of the meal he asked about the students he had picked. They were doing well. Beaufort smiled complacently.

"Tell me," he asked, "how's Jock Baird getting on? He was the best of the bunch."

One of the instructors shook his head sadly. "Jock is the only bad apple in the lot."

"How's that?"

"He's quite mad."

"He's *what?*" roared Beaufort.

"Ask Captain Mackenzie. Jock has been under his care."

"Yes," put in Mackenzie, "he's lost his mind. Pity. He was such a nice chap, you know. Cracked up under the strain."

"And what steps are you taking to handle the case?" Beaufort demanded.

"I'm afraid I know very little about psychiatry, Major Beaufort. I'm only a G.P. We thought you might be so kind as to give us advice. He became so violent that we had to lock him up."

"My good man! Lock him up! You certainly know nothing about psychiatry. Where can you keep him in Arisaig? You have no hospital. This whole set-up is medieval! What have you done with him?"

"Well, we put him in one of the cell blocks near the gardener's house. The cell block is stone and old and cold, I admit, but Bonnie Prince Charlie slept there one night. Jock has only been there for two days. We really had to put him away. He thought we were plotting against him and he would punch and scratch and bite. He bangs his head against the wall and bites his chains."

"Dreadful! Dreadful!" stormed Beaufort. "Take me to poor Jock at once."

It was as bad as he feared. Jock was chained to the wall as if in a dungeon, his clothes tattered, his hair matted. He would scream, roll his eyes, bare his teeth, and spit through the bars at the visitors. Beaufort began to speak to him in a soothing voice. "Jock, remember me? I'm your friend. My name's Major Beaufort. I'm your friend, Jock, I'm your friend."

Jock stopped spitting and cringed into a corner. "Open the door," said Beaufort, "I'm going in."

"I say, old man, isn't that a bit risky?" protested Captain Mackenzie.

"Open the door, Captain."

Mackenzie obeyed and Beaufort stepped in, all the while droning his hypnotic "I'm your friend." Step by step he moved toward Jock.

"I am your friend. I want to help you. I will get you out of here. You must believe me, Jock. I am your friend."

Finally he reached Jock and sat down beside him, still keeping up the flow of soothing words. He put his arm around Jock's shoulder, and with his other hand stroked Jock's hair, his face, his brow. Jock, like a wounded dog licking his master's face, began to pet and stroke Beaufort's right arm. It was a touching sight. He tenderly cradled the arm in his hands. He examined it inch by inch from wrist to elbow. He nestled his face again it. Suddenly he sniffed, growled, and buried his teeth in the flesh. Beaufort sprang to his feet with a yell of pain and dashed out of the cell crying:

"The fool! The fool! He is mad!"

The staff was so sympathetic and solicitous about his injured arm that Beaufort's suspicions were aroused. Late that night he crept past the sentry down the path to the cell block. His suspicions were confirmed. Jock was not there!

A number of Jeds came to Arisaig for training, and they were the most obstreperous of all. Jeds were three-man teams who dropped behind the lines in France to help organize the resistance movement. One member of each team was American, one British, one French. The story of their gallant exploits has been told in part in *Sub Rosa* by two former Jeds, Stewart Alsop, the well-known political columnist, and Tom Braden. I had been sent to England as a Jed, but before I began training my unlucky papers caught up with me in London.

When the plans for these teams were first drawn up, someone said, "We need a cover name for this operation." One of the planning officers, so the story goes, glanced at a map of Scotland which happened to be lying on the table. His eye fell on a small Lowland town and he suggested, "How about calling it Jedburgh?" So "Operation Jedburgh" became the official name. The town itself is pronounced

"Jedbruh," but some Americans, under the impression they were being very very correct, called it "Jedborrow." Others tried "Jedberg," or "Jedbird," but most of us simply said "Jed."

The very qualities for which Jeds were picked—courage, initiative, resourcefulness—made them a hard bunch for the instructors to handle. I heard about them from the Adjutant at Arisaig, Captain Godfrey, a well-known London banker and bachelor-about-town. He had fought in World War I and was fifty-one years old when World War II broke out, but he promptly joined up again. Godfrey told stories of the fabulous Loch Ness sea-monster, which sober witnesses swore they had seen in broad daylight, and of the Hebridean islands, Eigg and Rum and Uist and Iona, where Saint Columba landed in his coracle. He also told me tales of the Jeds.

Their worst problem-Jed was an enormous Swede from Minnesota named Gus Christiansen, a professional football player. I had known Gus in London. We nicknamed him the Big Ass Bird, because he was such a slow starter, but he could be quick enough when he chose.

Once Gus and another Jed, named Mertz, were dining at the Officers' Club in Grosvenor Square, when they noticed a famous face at another table.

"See that Navy Commander over there?" said Mertz eagerly. "That's Jack Dempsey."

"Yeah," agreed Gus in a bored tone.

"Gee! I wish I could meet him."

"Well, hell," said Gus, "let's go over and I'll introduce you."

He lumbered up to Dempsey and swatted him on the back with the flat of his hand and all the force of his two hundred and fifty pounds. Dempsey choked, and leaped to his feet ready for trouble. There stood Big Gus grinning amiably, with his ham hand outstretched. Dempsey, bewildered but always a sportsman, shook it.

"Hi, Jack, remember the last time we met?" Dempsey looked blank. "It was in the locker-room of the Chicago Bears when I was playing pro ball for the Wisconsin Badgers."

"Of course! Of course!" cried Dempsey, greatly relieved, and the two big men laughed and kidded one another. Then Gus said:

"Say, Jack, I want you to meet my pal, Ray Mertz."

Dempsey shook hands with the awed Mertz, and after the exchange of a few more pleasantries the two Jeds returned to their table.

"Christ, Gus, I didn't know you knew Jack Dempsey that well. You never told me about it."

"I don't know him at all," answered Gus calmly, "but you wanted to meet him, didn't you? It makes no difference to Dempsey whether I know him or not. He's met millions of people and always glad to meet a few more."

In Scotland Gus and two other Americans were assigned the task of overcoming and disarming a sentry on guard duty. A local Home Guard unit was stationed in a castle nearby and the Home Guard sentry at the castle gate was to be the victim. Of course he was not warned, but the Americans were ordered not to hurt him or rough him up too much. Meanwhile their instructors would conceal themselves close at hand and rate them for speed and smoothness of performance.

Gus was by far the strongest of the three. It was agreed among them that he would jump the guard and the others would then help to hold the man until the instructors emerged from their hiding-place. To avoid notice they arranged to walk to the castle by different routes and meet at a point near the guard's post.

Gus arrived. After waiting ten minutes for his friends he grew tired of waiting and decided to do the job by himself. The sentry, a very young man, was proudly marching his post in a military manner. Gus lumbered up, holding out an unlighted cigarette.

"Got a match?"

The guard dug into his pocket and brought out a pack of matches, then stood at attention with both hands gripping the rifle in front of his chest while Gus lighted his cigarette. Gus handed back the matches to him and the guard stretched out his right hand to take them. In a flash Gus snatched the rifle out of the man's left hand.

"Little boys shouldn't play with guns," he remarked.

The astonished sentry glared at Gus.

"I say, Lieutenant, I'm on guard duty. Give me back my rifle."

"Tough luck, bub. You lost and I win. Where the hell are the others? No, don't you try and grab it back or I'll have to club you."

He yelled for the instructors to come out of hiding and get the problem over with. The sentry, now certain that he had fallen into the hands of a lunatic, blew his whistle, and the Captain of the Guard at the head of a platoon of infantry came dashing to the rescue.

"He won't give me my rifle," cried the sentry.

"But you lost, didn't you?" shouted Gus.

The platoon encircled Gus and was slowly closing in for the pounce when his two team-mates rushed up.

"Where have you been, you big dumb—— We've been waiting half an hour for you. This is the wrong place."

The Home Guard were indignant about the incident and it took all Godfrey's tact to pacify them. Their parting words were:

"All right, we'll let it go this time. But next time you let loose any of your crazy Americans on us we'll shoot them."

As a part of their training all Jeds had to learn to live off the land without help from outside. The first batch of Jeds who came to Arisaig, twelve Americans, were packed off to a nearby island. After two weeks of rugged outdoor training on the island the twelve were herded into a boat and put ashore on a bleak and lonely stretch of coast.

"These are your instructions," they were told. "Exactly one week from today you must meet us at this spot and we shall take you back to the island. Until then you are on your own. Live off the land as best you can."

"This is a dirty deal," protested the Jeds.

The instructor replied that life behind the lines would be even more uncomfortable.

"Give us just one gun and one knife between us to hunt game."

They were given no tools or weapons, in spite of their entreaties. Instead they were reminded that they must now put into practice the lessons they had learned in theory about living off the land. At last they slouched sullenly off as the British instructors veered their boat back towards the island.

The instructors returned, as arranged, a week later, expecting to find the Jeds with clothes tattered by brambles, shoes caked with mud, faces haggard and bearded, and tempers on edge. There stood the twelve Americans, sleek and cheerful, smoking fresh cigarettes, and greeting their instructors in the most friendly way. Something had gone wrong with the problem!

In fact, the Jeds had long ago guessed that the British would some day pull this kind of trick on them. So each man carried hidden on his body wherever he went a small compass, a detailed map of the area, and all the money he could save. When the British finally dumped them on the coast they were not surprised, and their protests were just a matter of form. As soon as the instructors had sailed away out of sight the Jeds put their maps together, located their position, which was eleven miles from Arisaig, and decided to spend the week at the Arisaig Hotel. With the help of the compass they reached the nearest road, hitched a wagon ride to town, checked in at the hotel, shaved and bathed and went down to the lounge for cocktails.

They spent a delightful week eating, drinking, reading, listening to the radio, playing poker. The better poker players among them soon had all the money but they readily loaned it back, so that no one suffered for lack of food or drink and the more foolhardy could reinvest their borrowings in another poker game. All twelve men gained weight.

Instead of worn, dispirited bushmen waiting on the shore, the British found happy holiday-makers.

"It wasn't quite cricket for the Jeds to do that," Godfrey added, "but we learned. Before we sent out the next batch to live off the land we stripped and searched them and gave them freshly laundered clothes. We also warned the local inhabitants and police that a band of dangerous Nazi saboteurs, speaking English and posing as American soldiers, was known to have landed on the coast. You know, Morgan, this made the problem quite realistic for your bloody American friends."

15 · Getting Closer

No SOONER was I back at Pemberley than I began to make plans for going to other schools. I felt that training would improve my chances of going to France. Within a week my plans were very nearly shattered for good.

One night I was Officer of the Guard, and returned to my room about seven in the morning. I snapped off my belt and holster and flung it on the bed. Of course I ought to have pulled the .45 pistol from the holster, removed the clip and cleared the chamber, but I just didn't bother. I was hanging up my blouse in the closet when Lieutenant Meldrum, an MTO and a good friend of mine, came into the room, whisked out the pistol, and primed it. I had my back to him and I realize now that I should calmly have said, "The pistol is loaded," but instead I whirled around to face him. He had me covered, only eight feet away, with the pistol pointing at my belly.

Meldrum was playing a game. He was in a boxer's crouch, the approved position for rapid-firing. We had learned the stance from the fabulous pair, Fairbairn and Sykes; I from Fairbairn and Meldrum from Sykes. These two, at that time army instructors, had been Chiefs of Police in Shanghai for many years. In the human cauldrons of the Far East they had tested many methods of killing, and their books had worldwide fame. Their *Shoot to Kill, Unarmed Combat,* and *Knifework* were sold by the thousand to men in all the Allied forces. Fairbairn was an expert with pistol, rifle, knife, the edge of his hand, and a box of matches. The Fairbairn knife is now almost as famous as the Bowie-knife.

"And when you have no weapons," he would tell us, "throw sand in his eyes, throw anything at him, get him off his balance, and then pull his eyes out of their sockets. I hope you're not offended, gentlemen. Murder is my business."

But here was Meldrum in front of me, only eight feet away. If I tried to reach him I was sure he would playfully click the trigger and say, "I got you." I knew it was loaded. He didn't. My mind was racing. I could tell that in a moment he was going to pull that trigger and say, "Bang." I managed to cry out "DON'T!" just as he fired. The terrific noise of the .45 in that small room echoed throughout the building. My cry had jolted his aim and the bullet missed me by two inches and plunged into the floor by my right foot. Meldrum, white and shaken, mumbled the inevitable, "I didn't know it was loaded."

I pulled the pistol from his trembling hand and unloaded it and we went downstairs to look for the slug. It had gone right through the floor, ripped through the pillow and mattress of a bed on which, half an hour earlier, a candidate had been sleeping, bounced off a nail in the floor, ricochetted from the wall along with a chunk of plaster, and come to rest in the far corner of the room. Smythe threatened to court-martial us both for negligence in the care and handling of a weapon, but after a few days he softened and let us off with an unofficial reprimand. This narrow escape impressed on us both the first rule in handling firearms, "Don't point unless you mean to shoot. Don't shoot unless you mean to kill."

When a man eight feet away threatens you with a gun you are helpless, but there are half a dozen methods of disarming a man at close quarters. It always amuses me to see a gunman in a movie or on television brandish a pistol under the hero's nose or jab it into the small of his back, whereupon the hero meekly throws up his hands. As Alex once said to me:

"I'd really enjoy having a man pull a gun on me like that, just for the pleasure of taking it away from him."

Another common mistake is for the hero to assault the villain with clenched fists, a method of attack that often results in broken knuckles. A far deadlier blow can be dealt with the outer edge of the hand. You hold your fingers close together, thumb outstretched at right angles. This tenses the muscle ridge that runs between little finger and wrist. If you put the whole weight of your body behind the blow it can easily kill, especially if it strikes the victim on the larynx.

Many students in Fairbairn's unarmed combat course became enamored of this particular blow. They would practice hitting the edge of their hand against the table to harden the muscle, and go about smacking their buddies on the neck, arm or thigh to test their own power. At the end of the course the students were given a problem to see how they would apply their knowledge. The student was led to a closed door and told:

"This room is occupied by the Chief of the Gestapo. In order to gain entrance to this building you have submitted to a body search, so you have no weapon concealed on your person. Your mission is to kill the Gestapo Chief in his office and any others who may be there. As soon as you have done so, get out as fast as you can. Don't hesitate to use any weapon or tool whatever to help you."

Then the door was opened and the student was admitted as if to a cage.

Behind the desk sat the Gestapo Chief, a bloated sawdust dummy. Nine out of ten students walked up to him, leaned over the desk, and struck their favorite edge-of-hand blow at his throat. The desk was too wide for the blow to be effective, and they had to run around and strangle him from behind. A live Gestapo Chief would have leaned back out of the way of the blow, pulled out a pistol and plugged his assailant as he ran around the desk.

Only one student in ten noticed the whopping shillelagh lying on the desk. Grabbing this he was able to conk the Gestapo Chief no matter how far he leaned back. Even when closet doors swung open and other dummies came racing out on pulleys most students went on busily hacking away with the edges of their hands until they were knocked down by the impact of the heavy bags of sawdust or were forced to jump out of the window to escape. Only a few had the presence of mind to use the shillelagh or a chair as a weapon, or to mash the dummies' heads together. Those who failed were given a second try at the problem and as a rule they learned from their previous mistakes and did very well.

This is an instance of what psychologists mean by saying, "Transfer of training must be specific." In other words, if you are teaching a man how to act in an emergency you must not merely rely on general principles and trust to him to adapt them to the occasion. Instead you must train him to meet many different kinds of emergency so that he develops specific habits to meet each one.

For the next month I worked assiduously at Pemberley. I was lucky in having only French candidates that month. Then I made my next move. It was mid-April and I had taken no leave since I joined the staff in November, so I asked to spend a week's leave at another training school. I was sent to Shipworth in the Midlands where I had training along the same lines as in the Scottish schools. Wrestling had been my chief sport in high school and college so that I was able to skip the courses in unarmed combat, which were mainly wrestling. I spent the extra time on weapons firing and demolitions.

The day after I returned to Pemberley Smythe sent me dashing up to London, to see a Major Bailey. I had no idea what I was to see him about. Bailey merely sent me on to a Colonel Olds, who in turn sent me on to see a Major Clubb at the top secret British Intelligence Headquarters which was, most appropriately, in Sherlock Holmes' Baker Street. As I walked towards the entrance a big-boned, shaggy civilian accosted me and said with a smile, "I say, you are

Leftenant . . . Leftenant . . . I say, I seem to have forgotten your name."

"Morgan."

"Oh yes, of course, how silly of me. My name's Clubb. I hope you won't mind my not being in uniform. Would you care to take a turn with me, Leftenant?"

As we strolled around the block he told me that one of the Assessment Boards, at Heathfield, near London, had been failing a high proportion of O.S.S. men who were first-generation Americans or of Jewish descent. Was the Board justified or was it biased? Many of the men whom this Board had rejected as psychological warfare officers were well-known—Hollywood screen-writers, New York advertising men, best-seller authors. It smelled. Was I willing to make a secret investigation of the matter? At my own risk? Very well then, a car would pick me up at my hotel and drop me off at Heathfield. Five days later the same car would return me to my hotel. I was to tell the driver nothing except my name. I was to tell the Heathfield officials only that I was studying British assessment methods.

"Good luck, old chap. When you have written your report, put it in a double envelope and hand it to Colonel Smythe. Don't tell him my name or anything about the mission. Don't do anything else about this affair unless I ask you to, and please don't mention my name to *anyone*."

The Heathfield Board was atrocious. Without evidence it was rejecting foreign-born Americans, Americans with un-English names, and Jews. The Commanding Officer brushed my questions aside with, "We understand these people much better than you Americans do. They have

only recently left Europe and they are much closer to us."
I sent in a damning report. I wonder if it ever did any good?

The time for the invasion of Europe was drawing near, though none of us at Pemberley knew the day it would take place. I was offered the chance of going into France as a counter-intelligence agent with the invasion forces. As our armies overran enemy territory I would interview our agents who had been working there, to find out whether they had remained loyal to us throughout their long stay behind the lines. I begged off the assignment. It called for a command of the subtleties and nuances of the French language which I did not possess.

16 · The Monastery

IN THE last two weeks of May only a trickle of candidates came to Pemberley. Our work was about done. We had a group of Frenchmen, and I suggested to Smythe that I accompany them to their training school in Sussex. Smythe knew what I was up to, but he was a reasonable man, and he let me go.

The Maquis School was housed in a fourteenth-century priory, or monastery, in Sussex. It was built by the monks themselves, of solid stone, but some later owner had added an incongruous wing of red brick. The Chief Instructor in this ancient building was, appropriately, a Shakespearean actor. His name was Vincent and he was a crack shot and a first-class beer-drinker. At the end of the course our class bought him a silver mug with a penny under glass at the bottom.

At the monastery we learned how to read maps, blow bridges, cut railroad ties, frisk suspects, and arrange recognition signals. We were also instructed in briefing and de-briefing and the use of the Sten, Bren, Marlin, Tommy, carbine, .45, .32, bazooka and Piat. The course included a number of situation problems, more extended and exacting than those at Pemberley. Some of these problems were carried out at night.

Our first night problem was to enter the heavily guarded monastery and remove a document—supposedly a Gestapo plan for crushing local opposition—from a desk in the drawing-room. Once the plan was in our hands the problem was over. We did not have to fight our way out again. Even so, we ran some risk, for we were forbidden to beat up or otherwise mistreat the unsuspecting guards, while they were quite likely to shoot any intruder or clobber him over the head. To make things harder for us, the instructors drove us out in a lorry ten miles from the monastery and let us off half an hour before sunset on a lonely farm road. Too late it occurred to us, as we watched them drive off, that we could have seized the lorry and driven back, leaving the instructors to hike the ten miles.

As usual, we had been instructed to keep out of sight of passers-by, so we left the road and walked along the hedgerows through the fields. As darkness fell we stepped into bogs of mud, bumped into trees, trod on fallen branches whose crackle alarmed the standing cattle and scattered them mooing in all directions. Two of the students who were rather nervous tried to persuade the rest to crawl all the way on their bellies. At that rate we should have taken a week to reach the monastery and arrived plastered with cowdung.

As we plodded along we discussed how we could enter the building. The French students were set on entering by a window. I was against it, because the monastery windows were shut every night and, like all windows in blacked-out England, so heavily curtained that, even when the light was on inside, it was impossible to see from outside whether anyone was in the room. But the students had an *idée fixe* about the window and refused to consider any alternative.

The drawing-room was on the first floor so they decided to force an entry through one of the windows in the dormitory above, on the chance that the instructors would not be guarding the second floor. One man remembered seeing an extension ladder in the repair barn. I pointed out the difficulty of carrying it unseen and unheard to the main building, and also the likelihood that the instructors would guess our reasoning and be waiting for us on the second floor. I asked leave to go ahead and scout the area, but the leader of the group had a better idea. I was to constitute myself a one-man mission to capture the document, while the rest followed their ladder-and-window plan. In this way the group's chances of success were doubled.

I set off at a brisk walk along the road towards the monastery, which was still eight miles distant. There was no moon but my eyes had grown used to the darkness and I walked almost as fast as in daylight, in spite of occasional painful jars when I stepped into potholes in the road. Half a mile from my destination I began to keep close to trees and bushes, and to watch for sentries and listen for footsteps.

The grounds were enclosed by a red brick wall, a foot thick and covered with vines. The gate was guarded day and night, and sentries constantly patrolled the wall. To reach the building I had to pass within this cordon of guards. Grasping the vines I slowly worked my way to the top of the wall and peered over. A dense hedge screened me from behind, and for ten minutes I stayed on the wall and scanned the grounds, but I could see nothing that looked like a sentry. So I eased myself down on the inside. There was no invisible sentry waiting to blow my head off, and I made my way very cautiously and noiselessly towards the main building. Sometimes I walked crouching over like a chimpanzee, sometimes I wriggled forwards on my belly. I contrived always to keep some bush or tree between me and the building until I reached the monastery graveyard, where I could hide behind the tombstones. The British had certainly not wasted any granite or marble in that graveyard. The stones were no bigger than head-markers in a military cemetery. A brick pathway led through the graveyard and across the lawn to the front door of the monastery. Suddenly I heard the unmistakable "clop-clop" of hobnailed boots smacking on the bricks. A sentry. Was he after me? I froze behind a laurel bush as he marched by, and then resumed my creeping progress. Fifteen minutes later he clopped past again. This must be his beat.

Instead of going straight towards the monastery, I began to move in a circular direction which would bring me around to the front of the building. All the while I was turning over in my mind possible ways of entering it, but none seemed promising. Outside the front door was another brick walk leading to a circular driveway, and in the middle of the circle was a clump of shrubs. I inched my way to this clump and concealed myself there. Now I could watch the front door and the sentries walking their beats and stopping to exchange a few words as they passed each other.

So far so good, but what was I to do next? For half an hour I lay in the shrubbery and tried to devise a way of entering the monastery unseen. The stretch between me and the front door was in full view of the guards and without a patch of cover.

As I lay fishing around in the depths of my mind for an answer I brought to the surface a piece of advice that Colonel Vincent had given us:

"Always try the obvious way first. Look for the key under the doormat. Don't be furtive. Don't climb in at a window when the door is open, however illegal your entry may be."

Just then a whistle blew. Had I been spotted by the sentries? Or had they seen the rest of my group? I did not think so. I had left the group three hours ago, and at their laborious pace they could scarcely have caught up with me yet. "Clop-clop, clop-clop, clop-clop" went six pairs of heavy British boots as six sentries assembled in front of the door, presented arms, lined up in twos and marched into the house. It was the changing of the guard. As far as I could see not a single sentry remained outside.

The plan flashed into my mind. I knew exactly what I was going to do. It was as simple as Vincent's advice. I stole quickly up to the house and flattened myself behind a brick projection in the wall alongside the front door. Next moment six guards walked smartly out of the door and down the pathway. As the last two guards went past me I stepped out, caught the door before it slammed shut, and slipped inside.

To my right along the corridor lay the open door of the guardroom. I walked past it. No one challenged me. Quickening my pace, I turned left into another corridor and flung open the drawing-room door. All the instructors were sitting there with drinks in their hands. I waved my pistol at them.

"Don't move! Don't make a sound!"

Still keeping my pistol pointed at them, I walked over to the desk and picked up the "Gestapo Plan," which was neatly spread out there.

"Okay, Morgan, your side wins. But where are the others?"

I explained that I was a one-man advance unit of the team, and was about to set off to tell the others that the problem was over, but the instructors deterred me.

"Don't spoil it for them; it isn't fair. Let them have a chance too. They may have a good plan."

So we all sat up and waited, and waited. At half-past three we heard whispering and scuffling on the lawn outside. A few moments later there was a crash of splintering glass upstairs followed by an agonized scream, "*Non! Non! NON!*" and then a heavy thud on the lawn. We all rushed out through the French window. The team had stuck to their misguided plan of forcing an entry through the dormitory window on the second floor. The sleepers there were awakened by the crash of glass and one of them, a British sergeant, ran to the window and shoved the ladder, man and all, away from the window and sent it toppling down onto the grass. Mercifully the Frenchman fell clear of the ladder and was only bruised and shaken.

Why have I described in such detail a long-ago wartime training problem? Am I trying to glorify myself, and show how much cleverer I was than those naïve Frenchmen? Far from it. The point I am trying to make is this. Wars come and wars go, but the mechanisms of the human intellect do not change. When faced with a practical problem our minds work in much the same way whether we are organizing a resistance movement or any other enterprise. My training as a psychologist had taught me the basic principles of learning and also the importance of first-hand observation. At Pemberley I was able to watch dozens of men and women tackling all sorts of practical problems. Different men will find different solutions, but the technique of successfully solving a problem is always basically the same.

First, the ground is thoroughly explored. Then there is a period of casting about in the mind for possible answers. It is important to keep flexible—not to freeze onto the first solution that offers itself. The French team thought first of the window plan and fell so much in love with it that they were blind to its defects. The mind must grope around, feeling this way and that, testing solutions and discarding them until the right one is found. It is no use trying to hurry. Before attempting to enter the monastery, I made a very careful reconnaissance and then spent some time thinking over the problem. I managed to solve it, not by any flash of genius but by patience and good luck.

The same advice came in handy on another problem, in which messages had to be passed from one man to another at a meeting-place, a hut on the local golf course. Some students would creep and crawl all over the fairway, and even crouch for hiding in bunkers at the risk of being hit by a golf ball. There was a policeman patrolling the road which ran across the course, and the students seemed drawn towards his beat like moths to a candle. Our team, on the contrary, made no effort to slink about unobserved. We dressed up in sports clothes, hired or borrowed bags of clubs, and strolled openly over the course without arousing the least suspicion. It was another instance of walking in through the front door.

The French students were very kind to me. Since I was older and more experienced they gave me carte blanche to act as a one-man team in the group's interest whenever I felt like it. In this way I was able to try out my own ideas even if they did not appeal to the group, while they learned from their own successes and mistakes without any short-circuiting from me. Vincent was not told of this informal agreement, which he probably would not have approved. At any rate, he began to grow more and more irritable towards me. Late one afternoon he briefed us on the evening's problem—to blow up a motor pool. The demolitions, he said, were already in our possession, carefully cached underneath a wooden trapdoor which opened from the orchard on to a stairway leading down to the monastery cellars. The motor pool itself was only half a mile away, but we were to be driven in a lorry to the nearest town, eight miles off, receive detailed instructions there, walk back to the monastery, pick up the demolitions and go on to the motor pool. The pool was closely guarded, and we were to use great caution there, but until we reached it, Vincent assured us, we should expect no difficulty.

Somehow this briefing had a fishy smell. I wondered if Vincent were hinting that we ought always to expect the unexpected. And I was not especially anxious to tramp eight miles in the dark through wheat and barley fields if I could help it. So immediately after dinner I slipped away through the shadows of dusk to the orchard. For a while I hid behind an apple tree and peered this way and that in search of a guard. Seeing none, I crept on all fours, as fast as I could without making any noise, through the long grass until I reached the trapdoor. Very slowly I eased my hand under the edge of the trapdoor and felt around for the demolitions. They were there, all right, and by fingering them gently I discovered that they were in a bag tied by wire to a beam underneath the trapdoor. It looked as though the instructors had tricked us by wiring the bag. If so, the mechanism would be either push or pull, more likely the latter, since a man grabbing the bag would naturally pull it towards him. I had no wire-clippers so I tried to break the wire by twisting it back and forth, not knowing whether the booby-trap would be an electric shock, a horrendous noise, a fragmentation grenade or a gun shooting me. The Maquis School played rough. I broke one wire and had to hold up the bag—a good twenty pounds—with my right hand while I twisted the remaining wire with my left. I must have jerked it, for suddenly there was a loud explosion about thirty feet behind me, startling me out of my skin and showering me with dirt and stones. In the brief bright light of the explosion I saw a soldier running towards me. I gave one final tug at the demolitions bag, but it stayed firm, so I let go of it and began to run, bent double, from one tree trunk to another until I reached a side entrance to the monastery and ducked inside. Meanwhile students and instructors were galloping out of the back door and into the orchard. Most of them thought that enemy planes had dropped a small bomb. I found the dormitory empty except for one Frenchman lying on his bed. He looked me over and asked coolly, "Was it you, Morgan?" I told him it was, but that he, of course, understood that I had been in the dormitory all the time. "Entendu," he replied. In a few minutes the students streamed back, and with them Colonel Vincent and the soldier whom I had glimpsed in the orchard. "Was it him?" cried Vincent, pointing dramatically at me. "I couldn't say, Colonel. It was dark and he was running. I didn't spot him while he was working on it." Vincent was furious. "Morgan, you're the only one who would pull a dirty dodge like this. I know it, because I've worked with you bloody Americans and this is the kind of thing that only a Jed would do. You did it!" He appealed to the Frenchman, who at first seemed unable to grasp what all the fuss was about, but finally grunted, "Why are you yelling? He's been up here ever since dinner."

I was herded into the lorry with the others, Vincent abusing me all the while and calling me a yellow-bellied rat and a number of other names. Just as we were ready to start, I lost my temper and shouted back, "You Boy Scout! You claim to be teaching us to use our wits, and

Alex

Édouard—taken at the end of the Maquis Campaign

Jim on left, Claude on right—dressed up in their conference clothes

Bébé wears the tie. The man on the left was Bébé's mechanic, who saw to it that Bébé could always drive his car in the French tradition

Claude, and members of his Headquarters Staff

Men of the Maquis

Many were called, but few were chosen. They all volunteered.

The Russians are in front

German (Polish) POW in front of our "barracks"

He hated the Nazis

My bodyguard rides the fender

Lagic, François, Handlebar Hank, and another Croat at Lagic's home in Varennes

Close Shave

After the Germans got through with Oradour-sur-Glane

NAME OF BEARER.

Lieutenant W.H. Morgan

SUPREME HEADQUARTERS ALLIED EXPEDITIONARY FORCE.

Assistance to Allied Forces.

The bearer of this document is a regular member of the Allied Forces under the command of General Eisenhower whose object is the liberation of your territory from the enemy.

It is required that you should give such members of the Allied Forces any assistance which they may require and which may lie within your power, including freedom of movement, provision of information, provision of transport where possible and provision of food and shelter.

The Supreme Allied Commander counts upon your assistance in carrying out his wishes as expressed above, which are hereby endorsed by the French High Command.

By command of General Eisenhower.

Signed: ....
KOENIG

General Commanding
Forces Françaises de l'Intérieur.

Eisenhower says so (but it's J not H)

> **FORCES FRANÇAISES DE L'INTERIEUR**
> Corps Francs Libérateurs   IV° République
>
> ## CERTIFICAT
>
> Le Lieutenant de Parachutistes américains, WILLIAM J. MORGAN, commandant un détachement de volontaires du bataillon ANNE,
>
> certifie que le volontaire
>
> fait partie du Corps Franc ALEXANDRE depuis le 1° Septembre 1944.
>
> Signature du Lieutenant américain.   Signature du Titulaire.

The men earned this

> **Forces Françaises de l'Intérieur**
> R. 3. D. 5/2.   Bataillon ANNE
>
> Les Commandants ANNE et EDOUARD
>
> à Lieutenant ALEXANDRE,
> Lieutenant FRANÇOIS,
> Sous-Lieutenant SCHŒLCHER,
>   *Chefs de Corps Francs.*
> et à leurs Officiers, Sous-Officiers et Soldats.
>
> Les Commandants EDOUARD et ANNE, sont heureux de vous adresser leurs félicitations pour le bon travail que vous avez accompli dans votre secteur.
>
> Par votre courageuse conduite, vous avez été un exemple pour tous vos camarades.
>
> C'est à tous les braves qui, dans toute la France, ont mené comme vous la lutte avec ardeur, que notre Patrie doit sa libération rapide. Vous avez mérité la reconnaissance du pays.
>
> Le Bataillon est fier de vous.
>
>   P. C., le 12 Septembre 1944
>
> Commandant EDOUARD,   Commandant ANNE.

Alex and I got this

when we do, you squawk, 'It's not cricket!' Of course I did it. Why didn't you guard the place? Why don't you go yell at your guard for being asleep on duty?" We were still shouting at each other when the lorry drove away.

An instructor travelled with us to the town of Midhurst and gave us some further briefing about the motor pool before he dropped us off. As we trudged back across the fields I reflected that Vincent would be determined to catch me as soon as I appeared on the scene, so I worked out a plan with the others whereby I would be the decoy. When we reached the monastery grounds I took off my socks, put them on over my shoes, and I crept stealthily across the orchard. Two of the Frenchmen followed about fifteen feet behind me, with even greater stealth. As I reached the trapdoor, Vincent and another instructor sprang out at me with drawn guns. I stood up straight, flung up my hands and cried, "Don't shoot, don't shoot! You've got me. I surrender!"

Big grins overspread the faces of Vincent and his companion. They called a third instructor to come over and look at Morgan, the smart operator who had been caught red-handed. I was ordered to walk to the house.

"But I can't see very well," I complained. "Can't one of you lead the way?"

They merely laughed at my obvious ruse and flashed their flashlights on the path ahead of me. I slowed down in the hope that one of them would overtake me so I could try to snatch his weapon, but a voice behind me said, "Hurry up, Morgan. We know all the tricks. Don't try to get funny with us." They walked me up to the door of an old repair shop. I knew this place. It was cluttered with old paint cans, boards and saws. There was only one small window, no light, and five steps leading down from the door. I refused to go in, protesting that I would break my neck in the dark. The other two instructors walked off, apparently bored with the argument, and left me arguing with Vincent. He commanded me to enter, so I pushed the door inwards, while I grumbled that it would be the worse for him if I broke my neck. Vincent was close behind me. I pretended to stumble over the threshold and cursed Vincent loudly as I slipped behind the door. He took a step in after me and I slammed the door in his face with all my might, knocking the flashlight out of his hand. I heard it break on the ground. I bolted the door on the inside, ran across to the window, which to my astonishment was unbolted, climbed out, ran across the grounds, and joined my group at the motor pool. Everything had gone smoothly for them. The two Frenchmen who followed me had removed the demolitions bag without trouble. They had wire-cutters ready, but the bag had not been wired.

The French students had gained experience and confidence since the early problems. They had devised an ingenious plan for dealing with the sentries at the motor pool. Two men fired revolvers on one side of the pool and a few moments later two more men fired on the other side. The sentries were distracted by this double diversion and it was easy for the rest of us to enter the pool and "blow it up," that is, blow the tread off a derelict tank.

When we returned to the monastery Vincent greeted us

with jovial friendliness and congratulated us on a good performance. You would never have guessed there had been ill-feeling between us. And yet I am ready to swear that, actor as he was, his fury with me and his glee at my capture were not feigned. Did he decide he had been unfair to me, and deliberately let me escape from the shed? Or did the other instructors put pressure on him? I shall never be sure. As I say, he was an actor. But whatever his feelings, he played more than fair with me, as I shall tell later. I am inclined to think, as I look back, that his resentment of me stemmed in part from differences between American and British concepts of leadership. The leadership tests at Pemberley were of two types—leaderless problems like the Pond, where a leader would emerge from the group; and assigned-leader problems like the Madman, where a leader was designated by those in authority. The British, with their deep-rooted respect for law and order, were apt to look with some suspicion on an emergent leader. A useful type in the field, no doubt, but without the respectable status of an assigned leader—something of a ruffian, really. The British have the tradition of a governing class, who are actually assigned leaders. We are told that this tradition is now dying, but in 1944 it was far from dead, and I doubt if it is so today. In the United States the emphasis is different. The man who steps forward and takes the lead on his own initiative is apt to be more admired than the man who has it handed to him on a platter by a higher authority.

While I was in Sussex the Normandy Invasion was launched and the V-1's began streaking across the skies like planes on fire. I began to feel I was wasting time, and I told Vincent I had set my heart on going to the parachute school at Ringway. I told him that I would stand a much better chance of going into France if I could jump. Besides, as a psychologist I was curious to know what it felt like to leap out of a plane in defiance of basic instincts.

"I understand," said Vincent. "I wanted to go to France myself, but the red-tabs turned me down. I don't know what I can do for you, but I'll do my best."

On the last day of the course, a Saturday, he showed me a list of the men who were under orders to go to Ringway next day for jump training. All the other names were typed, but at the bottom of the list, in an almost undecipherable scrawl, was "Lieutenant W. J. Morgan." It was almost too good to believe.

"What shall I do?" I asked Vincent.

"Well, your name is there, isn't it?" he said. "Never mind how it got there. The only thing you can do is comply with military orders."

Late that afternoon I wired to my two superiors, Colonel Smythe at Pemberley and Major Bailey in London, "I have received military orders to proceed to Ringway within twenty-four hours. If I do not hear from you I shall assume that I must comply with these instructions and shall proceed as directed." It was Saturday evening and I rather thought that Smythe might not be at Pemberley nor Bailey at his Grosvenor Street office. But what else could I do? I had no other addresses for them. On Sunday there was still no wire from Smythe or Bailey. I waited till the last moment, then hurled myself and my duffel bag into the back of the truck among the cheering French students, who helped to pull me on board. "Allons, Guillaume, allons Reengway pour le parachutage." On the train we played "pokair," of which they were all very fond.

17 · Hook-up

Ringway was a cinch. On the first day we practiced with mock-up planes and jumped out of the holes; swung on risers from the loft of a high barn; jumped out of a hole in a balcony with our shoulder straps fastened to a cable above; and practiced getting out of the parachute harness. We watched movies showing what to do when dragged along the ground by a chute in a high wind, how to land in a lake or crash into a tree, and listened to talks by instructors, who answered our questions with calm assurance. The instructor for our group was a rugged young missionary of about thirty-two who had a church on the Gold Coast in Africa.

The second day we went up in a Lancaster. Our reverend instructor, who had made more than fifty practice jumps, went out first while still chit-chatting with us. It all seemed so easy. One after another we kicked ourselves out of the hole after him. It was the greatest thrill of my life. I jumped from the dark inside of the plane into the June sunshine. The slip stream pushed me clear of the plane; there was an upward tug as the chute opened. I looked up and there it was, swinging to and fro. I knew it was an illusion and I was doing the swinging. I would have liked to stay up there for an hour, but a booming voice from the microphone a few hundred feet below warned me:

"Okay, Morgan, good clean exit. Now, put your feet together, pull your risers to your chest, keep your chin on your chest, your elbows by your sides, don't get tense, roll when you hit the ground."

The grazing sheep below me began to run with the wind away from me as I descended on them.

The next day, Wednesday, we made our second jump, ten men to a plane, jumping in sticks of five, and on Thursday we did the same thing. I was Number 2 man at the hole —that is, the Number 1 man for our stick. Sitting opposite me across the hole was the Number 1 man, a smart young red-haired, red-moustached British lieutenant. Just as we were over a small town on our way to the drop field he swung his feet into the hole, placed his hands on the edge, stiffened his arms, and poised himself for the jump. He would break his neck if he landed in the street.

"Grab him!" I yelled, pointing at him. The man behind him clutched him by the shoulder straps and the sergeant dispatcher thrust his arms under Red's armpits so that he could not push himself out of the hole.

He kept struggling and screaming, "Let me go! Let me go!"

It was very frightening to us all. When we reached the drop zone he was still hysterical. The green lights and buzzers went on, the man behind him and the sergeant let go, and he vanished through the hole. I followed as fast as I could and landed a hundred feet from him.

"What the hell got into you, Red?" I asked.

"I don't know. I got too nervous. Felt I had to get out of that plane. It won't happen again."

It didn't. He finished the rest of his training at Ringway without so much as a twitch of the eyebrows.

On Friday afternoon we jumped with a 40-pound leg bag strapped to our legs, and late that evening we made our fifth and last practice jump, the night jump. I made a poor exit. In my anxiety to get out of the hole in the allotted half-second, I pushed too hard with my right arm. My body twisted as I went through the hole, the wind was high and the slip stream caught me. I began to somersault. I saw the lights of the field; then they disappeared. I saw them again, then they were gone again. What a predicament, somersaulting through the air with an unopened chute. I don't remember feeling any fear, but I do remember saying, "Well, I'll be goddammed." The lights went by again. "That makes three," I said aloud. Just then I felt the tug of a chute cord trying to get under my right arm. I followed instructions and kept my arms tightly by my sides, hands gripping my trousers. This was to prevent the risers and cords from breaking our arms in an emergency. But the cord was stronger than I. I had just finished saying, "No, you don't," when it whipped under my arm and lifted it above my head. I heard a crunchy snap, and the arm dropped limply to my side. "You stupid sonofabitch," I kept saying to myself as I worked frantically with my left hand, pulling the risers down to my chest and trying to control the now-opened chute. In the few seconds left I maneuvered so as to roll on my left side when I hit the ground. As I struggled out of the harness I went on cursing myself out loud.

"I say, old chap, something wrong? We heard you swearing at yourself in the air." Two British officers were beside me as I was trying to roll up my chute with one arm. One of them gathered up my chute and the other took me to the first-aid hut. The doctor found I had only a dislocated shoulder, not a broken arm, as I had feared. He gave me a sedative and snapped the joint back into place.

The next day, a qualified parachutist, with a total of five weeks' instruction in various phases of what is now called "unconventional warfare," I was on my way to London to look for an assignment.

First I went to see Major Bailey in Grosvenor Street, but he had gone "operational," as they say, and his former deputy, Captain Perkins, was sitting in his chair as Director of O.S.S. Schools and Training in the European Theater. I had known Perk for almost a year. When he went through Pemberley we had recommended that he be kept at a desk in London because of his remarkable talent for administration. He still bore us a grudge for it. He greeted me with:

"That was a dirty trick you pulled on me and Bailey, sending that telegram when you knew we wouldn't be in the office."

"Perk, for cat's sakes, I was only following military orders. One of you should have had the office covered. Where were you both? At Claridge's? You ought to be sorry for a guy with his arm in a sling."

"You should have broken your neck, you dope. As a matter of fact we had it all set to court-martial you as soon as you got to London, but when we heard you had hurt your arm we figured you got what was coming to you. Look, Bill, if you think you're going into the field, you're crazy. The French don't want us there. I know. I've been looking for an assignment myself. Nobody wants us. You've wasted your time with all that training. I can't help you, but let me know if you land a slot, and I'll go with you. I've got fifty men, all good instructors, and we don't have anything to do. We'll *all* go."

I thanked him, and went out to free-lance for a job.

London was full of O.S.S. brass. Where should I start? I went into a pub and fell into a conversation with an O.S.S. WAC. Over a beer mug I told her my troubles. "You ought to see George Wright," she said. "He's the one who gets things done in London." Wright, a Colonel in civilian clothes, listened carefully to my story and made an appointment for me to see a Major Gerard in Baker Street.

Gerard, I later learned, was in civilian life the manager of one of New York's most famous hotels. He was a handsome, ebullient man, with a French accent and a smooth manner. He seemed delighted to see me, and said he was in desperate need of French-speaking Americans to serve with the Maquis. It was the task of the Maquis to disrupt the German occupation forces and prevent them from holding up the Allied advance. They needed organizers, instructors, guerrilla leaders.

"Where do you want to go?" he asked me. "You can choose your spot."

"Look, Major," I said, "I don't know France. I don't speak French very well. It doesn't make much difference." I walked up to the big map of France on the wall, closed my eyes, and planted my forefinger somewhere on it. "Suppose I go there?" I asked, as I opened my eyes.

"Fine! Right in the center!" cried Gerard. "That's the Creuse. Very active area. Lot of fighting. They need help badly. You shall go there. I'll get you over in a couple of weeks. But right now I want you to go down to Donwell to take the straight intelligence course. Too many of our people get picked up. They know how to blow bridges and shoot guns, but they don't understand the finer points of intelligence or security. You'll need the course. Even though you'll be working with the Maquis, you'll have to go over in civilian clothes. Germans are all over the place."

I remembered Perk. "Major," I asked, "could you use as many as fifty men, well-trained Americans, some of them French-speaking?"

Gerard beamed. "Send them along to me. I've got jobs for all of them." He put on his glasses and went back to the piles of papers and cables on his desk.

Before I took the train to Donwell I went to see Perk. "I've got an assignment in France." He was out of his chair and clutching the lapels of my blouse. "Jesus Christ, how did you do it? Come on, Bill, tell me. I'm your pal." I told him that Gerard wanted him and his men. They had to get a special chute for Perk, who was well over two hundred and fifty pounds. He took all his best men along with him and left the Schools and Training Division without a Chief or even a Deputy. The whole Division office had to be reorganized.

The Donwell School taught the techniques of intelligence operations. By the time a student reached Donwell he was supposed to have learnt sabotage, subversion and guerrilla operations. At Donwell he acquired those skills which the popular mind associates with a spy. He learned how to recruit agents, steal and conceal documents, code and decode messages, use secret inks, tail a man and keep him under surveillance, and fabricate a cover story. My room-mate, Dave, was an Anglo-French Jew whose brother had been hanged as a spy by the Nazis. Dave wanted revenge. We worked together on a number of problems.

On one problem our instructions were to tail a woman who would get off the 9:30 train in a nearby city, and follow her about all day, even if she knew we were following her, until 4:30 in the afternoon. Then the three of us would meet at a hotel bar before returning to Donwell. We watched at the station and read the description we had been given: "Age twenty-five to thirty, height about five feet five inches, blonde, fair skin, stocky but not fat, sometimes wears glasses, not beautiful but might be called pretty." You have no idea how many women come near to answering that description. Dave and I were going to split up to follow the two most likely prospects when we spotted the right one stepping off the train.

She walked briskly out of the station and hopped on a bus. We followed in a cab. In the center of town she skipped off that bus and jumped on a crosstown bus coming at right angles. Our cab was caught in a traffic jam. Dave stayed to settle with the cabbie while I hopped on the bus. It moved slowly, and Dave ran ahead and flagged it down at the next corner. He took a seat in front of the girl while I stood at the rear. Just as the bus was starting up again, she upped and jumped off and disappeared into a crowd of shoppers. We frantically pushed our way off the bus, imploring the driver to stop. He must have thought we were sex maniacs or out of our minds. For an hour we scouted the area, walking the streets, peering into women's shops, searching the five-and-ten-cent store. Finally we gave up and decided to put in time in a cinema until the 4:30 rendezvous.

As we sat down in the darkened theater I glanced at the seat next to mine and there sat the blonde. What luck! Ten thousand places where she might have gone in this city, and here she was beside me. Dave and I nudged each other and grinned. Up she got, went down the aisle and into the women's room. I went to the right, into the foyer, Dave waited at the left in a darkened aisle. She came out and walked past Dave and out through an emergency door into an alley. Dave was right behind her, while the audience shouted for someone to close the door. I joined Dave in the tail on the street as they came out of the alley, and from then on she just could not shake us. We stayed on her tail, even in a fishmonger's shop, until 4:30, when the three of us walked arm in arm into the hotel bar for a Martini.

Dave took all the problems seriously. He was determined to get even with the Nazis for killing his brother. Sometimes, when the tension was tightest, he would explode with nervous laughter. One of the problems was to enter a strange house, search a room, find a hidden document, decode the message on the document and return to Donwell. To make the problem realistic, the instructor had hidden the document in a friend's study eight miles away while paying a social call. He had not, of course, told the friend and his family to expect visitors in a few days' time, so there was a good chance that this man or his neighbors might take a pot shot at us if they saw us prowling around.

Dave and I set out early in the afternoon, walking on the road when there was no risk of being seen, but keeping for the most part to the woods which lined the road. We had a detailed map of the area which enabled us to use all the available cover. When we reached the house we circled around to the rear, where our map showed a small stream in a gully, and waited in the gully for the rest of the afternoon. From time to time we would climb up the bank and peer through the brush at the house and its occupants. There were three of them, the owner, his wife, and the maid. The couple were sitting on the lawn facing us, while the maid brought out tea and sandwiches. It was growing dark. I went down the stream to the point where it was nearest to the house. The study was at this end of the house, with a door leading into the garden. Dave signalled that the coast was clear. I walked quickly to the house and in through the study door, unlatched two of the study windows and returned to the gully. No one had seen me.

Clouds came up. The couple went indoors. It began to pour. They shut all the windows and doors. Gloomily we saw the maid latch the windows I had taken so much trouble to unlatch, and lock the study door. We were soaking wet. It was hard to tell whether they had gone to bed, because in England during the war all houses were blacked out, but after a while we grew accustomed to the dark and could detect chinks of light. About ten o'clock the chinks disappeared. We shed most of our sopping clothes, wiped ourselves so that we would not drip on the floor, and walked around the house looking for the first-floor bathroom. We had guessed right. If there is one window in the house left open, it is the window above the toilet. We took off our shoes. Dave pushed me up to the window. I clambered in, and then pulled him up after me. We tiptoed through the dining-room, down a passage, and into the study, and locked the door behind us. Then we unlocked the door leading into the garden in case we had to make a quick getaway. As we began to search, Dave got the giggles. I knew the signs. In a few moments he would be laughing out loud in hysterics, and we would have to run out of the house and hide in the woods, with every chance of being caught. I clapped my hands over his mouth, but his eyes were twinkling with laughter and at any moment his guffaws would shake the house.

I switched my hands to his throat and began to choke him. In a few seconds he nodded his head and I released my grip. He coughed quietly, grabbed my hand, shook it, and muttered, "Thanks, Bill."

We wasted some time looking for the document in the hundreds of books in the study. We had orders to be out of the house by midnight. Just as we were beginning to become discouraged, Dave began inspecting the brickwork over the fireplace. Mortar was missing between two of the bricks. We probed the space with a nail-file and brought out a very small slip of paper bearing the message in code. We decoded it, relocked the outside door, tiptoed to the bathroom, scrambled out of the window. In the gully we put on our shoes and the rest of our wet clothes and began to work our way back to Donwell.

After walking two miles on the road we heard footsteps coming in our direction and hid in the woods. In spite of the darkness, we recognized the passers-by as two of our classmates. Afterwards we found that they had been on their way to the same house. Their job was to catch us. They made too much noise trying to pick a lock, lights went on all over the house, and the owner appeared in the doorway with a rifle in his hands, so they ran away.

At Donwell I learned how I had played a part in the life of a German agent, a Frenchman. During a lecture a picture was flashed on the screen showing the faces of two men who had tried to play the role of "double agent." In other words, working under instructions from the Germans they had tried to pass themselves off as willing spies for the Allies. The British rule in these cases was to give them all the rope they wanted until the hanging day arrived.

I recognized one of the double agents in the picture as a French candidate whom I had tested at Pemberley. He did not mingle with the others in his group, except occasionally with one member of the group. His story was that he had worked in an aviation factory in France and had engaged in minor sabotage by tossing parts into the wrong bins. He said that when he heard that he was to be sent to Germany as a slave laborer he escaped over the Pyrenees into Spain and thence to England. This was one of the more frequent escape routes from France. Several candidates had told me similar tales, but they were always proud of their feat and boasted how they had outwitted the Spanish guards at the border. This man told his story as though from memory without enthusiasm or bravado. Because of his aloofness he did poorly on the group situation tests. I was puzzled when, on the second day of this man's stay at Pemberley, Colonel Smythe came to ask me how he was doing. As a rule Smythe concerned himself only with candidates who were doing well or extremely badly. This man seemed, so far, to be a borderline failure.

"I'm not quite sure about him," I said. "He isn't doing very well, but I won't be sure for another two days. I'm never certain till the end."

"I'm interested in his getting through," said Smythe.

"Frankly," I replied, "if I had to bet right now, I'd bet against him. He seems to be a queer character with rather a fishy story, and the men in his group don't cotton to him."

"I hope you won't be too hard on him," said Smythe.

"Well, if I'm going to rely on my own judgment I can't promise that he will pass, but if you want him to pass regardless, suppose you put it as a military order?"

"All right, then," said Smythe, "if you wish it that way, you can take it as an order."

So in my report I had to let the man scrape through with a D rating, but I put in the report that I was skeptical of his story and didn't trust him.

Now I found out at Donwell that the doubts I had raised about this man had been raised by others before he came to Pemberley. The higher-ups in London had asked Smythe to let the man pass but had given no reason for their request. One of the other candidates in his group, the only one with whom he was at all friendly, was a British agent keeping a tab on his movements. By the time he had got through Pemberley and the various training schools they had evidence that he was an agent for the Germans operating through a radio network with a cut-out in London, where he went on week-ends whenever he was given leave. He was allowed to go through the Scottish schools, the jump school at Ringway, a course in industrial sabotage, and the two-week course at Donwell. All the time he was being watched. His Conducting Officer was also a British agent. Finally, when all his contacts were known, he was given his mission, briefed, and searched just before he stepped onto the plane. It was the rule to search any agent going into the field to make sure he was not carrying any giveaways—names and addresses, American cigarettes or English tailors' labels.

When the plane carrying the double agent reached the drop zone, the Sergeant Dispatcher made as if to hook up the static line and snap the cotter-pin in place. If the agent had remembered his lessons at Ringway he would have pulled hard on the static line to test it before he jumped. But like most men in such circumstances he was too nervous to think, and the Sergeant Dispatcher did not remind him. When he jumped from the plane he had, at most, ten seconds to live.

The moral of this story, as far as the British were concerned, was not that evil men were punished for their sins, but rather "Don't let a double agent know you've got the drop on him till you have no further use for him and are ready to destroy him."

When the lecture was over, I turned to speak to Domenic, the student who was sitting beside me. He was a tall, good-looking young man who came from a family of wealthy bankers in Rome, and through his family's influence he had become one of Mussolini's bodyguards. He had told me that after the war began he grew disgusted with the Fascist régime, fled from Italy, made his way to New York, and offered his services to O.S.S. Besides his native language he spoke French, English, and German. Now I saw that beads of sweat were standing out on his forehead.

"What's the matter, Domenic? Are you feeling ill?"

"Yes. Because now I know what they are going to do to me."

"Oh, no!" I said. "It's obvious you are not a double agent."

"They have no evidence that I am anything else. Everything they know about me and my motives for serving the Allied cause has come from my own lips."

For the rest of the course at Donwell he was a most unhappy man, in spite of all I could say to reassure him.

When the Donwell course was over I spent three days in London while the ends were tidied up. I was outfitted with two complete sets of French clothing. I was told my name would be "Marceau," and I would be on the "Murderer" circuit. I studied a detailed map of the Creuse. An Anglo-French agent who knew the area was sent to describe it to me and to work out a cover story for me. This was not easy. There was no hope of my passing as a Frenchman if I opened my mouth, so it was decided that if I were caught I would have to trust my own wits. Perhaps I could pretend to be insane.

The day I left, Gerard met me at a house in Wimpole Street. "If you can't make contact with our people in France," he told me, "you may, as a last resort, ask for '*Édouard, l'homme qui ne fume pas.*' Here's a hundred thousand francs for you. Don't worry about accounting for it. Here's three million for Édouard. Make sure he gets it." He handed me a letter of authorization from General Eisenhower, and shook my hand, pressing into my palm a pair of gold cuff-links in the shape of swastikas. "If you are caught," he said, "these may help to set you free. Good luck, Marceau."

18 · Action Station

13 AUGUST 1944. This was my day, my night. The invasion of Normandy was more than two months old, but the Allied armies were still struggling to break through the German defences, with the help of the Maquis, or French guerrillas. The Maquis were fiercely brave, but for the most part poorly trained and organized. Carefully chosen men and women were flown over from England and dropped in by parachute to act as guerrilla leaders and weapons instructors. During my months at Pemberley I had helped to select these leaders by the most rigorous standards. Now my turn had come.

I felt as though sentenced to the electric chair. In two hours parachute straps would be placed over my shoulders, around my waist and thighs—symbolizing to me the leg and arm straps of the electric chair in grey-walled Sing Sing prison. I had visited Sing Sing, and I once more smelled the dark corridors and saw the gloom on the prisoners' faces and their muscles twitching in anticipation of punishment. Mine were twitching now.

There were four of us in the car on our way to the airfield. Two of them were American bazooka experts going in on a second mission to destroy tanks. The third was a cocky young Frenchman, always chattering about sex, who was to join an espionage net near Paris. I remembered him well as a student in the assessment school and later at the Ringway jump school. There, after an exhausting day of parachute training, he would go out gallivanting with English girls every night.

I was to drop alone into the Department of the Creuse, in the central part of France. As I said earlier, an intelligence operator must be prepared for anything. The plan was to drop me into an area held by the Maquis, but with the German armies shifting rapidly about I might find myself in the midst of the enemy. I wore civilian clothes, just in case. If caught I would be shot, in or out of uniform.

As we rode along we tried to make conversation but it was stilted and abrupt. I was obsessed with a fear that my chute would not open. Regular paratroops wear a reserve chute, but they jump at a thousand feet or higher. I was to jump at four hundred feet, where a reserve chute would not open in time. So I had none.

Then at a crossroads our car was struck from behind by a British staff car and spun right around so that it faced in the opposite direction. We all sprang out to examine the damage, which was negligible. But, after that I was no longer nervous. Irrationally I felt that luck was with me. "Two accidents can't happen in the same day. In a few hours I'll be safe in France."

At the airfield I was met by an O.S.S. case officer, a former professor of French at a midwestern university. He zippered me into my earth-brown jump suit camouflaged with dark green splotches and provided me with a .32 and a .45 pistol, both loaded, a small flask of brandy, a map of France printed on thin silk, an axe, a small folding shovel, cigarettes and matches, and the inevitable K rations. I also had the wad of French money Gerard had given me. They were genuine francs, printed in England on stolen plates. All these things were stuffed into the roomy pockets of my jump suit, till I could scarcely walk for the bulges. As soon as I landed I was to rip off my suit, empty the pockets, dig a hole with the axe and shovel and bury chute and suit.

The case officer then introduced the air corps sergeant who was to be my dispatcher on the flight. He greeted me cheerfully with, "Here's your chute, I'll adjust it for you. You're a lucky man. Our plane is the first to go."

I shook hands with the crew and climbed into the plane, a B-24, and we left at exactly 9:41 P.M. We were supposed to arrive at thirty minutes after midnight. In the bomb bay instead of bombs there were about sixteen cylindrical containers, six feet long, filled with weapons, ammunition, and explosives. In the tail of the plane were half a dozen wooden boxes and wicker baskets, each twice the size of an orange crate. These held clothing and more weapons and ammunition. All were to be dropped out along with me. If the sergeant-dispatcher were careless, one of them might hit me in the air. Around the boxes were stacked bundles of leaflets, to be dropped on the way. The sergeant began tidying up and rearranging the bundles, talking as he worked. In ten minutes he asked me more questions than the British had asked during the whole time I worked with them, but he never waited for an answer.

First he showed me a picture of his girl and asked me with a wink, "Ain't she a bee-yoot?" Then he went on, "Help yourself to the apples and sandwiches, and I've got gum in my pocket. You want to put on the earphones and listen to the pilot talk to the navigator? He's funny. Gets in trouble with the CO, tells him where to get off, that's why he's only a first lieutenant. Say, you know something? We're flying in a B-24, I'm 24 years old, and this is our 24th mission. That's a lucky sign. Say Lieutenant, if you have to go, this is the place for it. Some people think it's the mouthpiece of a dictaphone. I always like to see them try to use it that way. How many times have you jumped? Me, I've jumped four times, wanted to know how it felt to the fellows I kicked out. Had to kick out a Frenchman once. The poor guy froze at the hole."

He kept me busy chewing gum, eating apples and sandwiches, and helping him to kid the pilot over the intercom until we were over the English Channel. The rear gunner had gone to check his equipment—"Pout-pout-pout, pout-pout-pout" went the familiar chatter of a fifty-calibre machine gun. Was a German plane on our tail?

"Sorry. Forgot to tell you. That's the rear gunner test-firing. He always does it over the Channel. You can sit down again. Nothing serious."

I settled back and, to occupy my mind, began rehearsing Gerard's instructions: "You will wear civilian clothes, but keep away from cities and villages. Your French won't pass.

You are to instruct, organize, and lead Maquis troops in the Department of the Creuse. Never tell anyone your real name. Never let anyone know that Marceau and Murderer are the same person."

Suddenly I was thrown off the box on which I was sitting. The plane had turned on its side and began a series of gyrations, climbing, diving, weaving, and bobbing. The containers were secure in the bomb bay, but the boxes were sliding about. I managed to clutch a bulkhead, and looked out of the windows. On all sides puffs of lights came on and off like fireflies in the night, and far below, red belches of flame were shooting upward. "What's on now, Sergeant?" I asked. He, too, was grabbing a bulkhead.

"Nothing. Don't worry," he said. "We're over Normandy. They're shooting flak at us. Must be American flak. Not even coming close. Krauts aim better."

On the way to the drop zone, whenever we came over a large French town or city, the Sergeant would open the camera hatch and toss out a batch of propaganda leaflets. "That's to fool the Krauts," he would say with a wink. "Makes them think we're just a propaganda plane."

At thirty minutes after midnight he told me that the pilot and navigator could not find the drop zone. There were all sorts of fires and lights down below, but none gave the right signals. We might have to return to London. I yelled at him, "Go tell the pilot to keep looking. I'm not going to go back and sweat out this trip all over again."

The Sergeant came back to say, "He'll keep looking for thirty minutes more."

At ten minutes of one the intercom phone rang. The

Sergeant answered it, leaned over and looked out of the jump hole, then turned around and exclaimed, "It's down below. Get yourself ready. We're going to run in."

I sat down and inched myself to the hole. The Sergeant hooked up the static line and I pulled on it to test it, remembering Domenic. The tail-gunner helped the sergeant to push the boxes and baskets nearer to the hole. "Good luck," said the gunner. "Thanks," I replied as I wet my lips with my tongue. I refused to look through the hole. Heights make me nervous. The big cylindrical containers in the bomb bay were to be released first, then I would jump, and then the boxes would be pushed out. The plane must make at least two passes over the drop zone to get rid of all the supplies.

The intercom buzzer began to ring madly. The red light over the jump hole was flashing. The Sergeant raised his right arm above his head and in the voice of a bull moose roared, "ACTION STATION!" I swung my feet into the hole and sat tense, looking up at the Sergeant on the other side of the hole. He gave me a wide smile for obeying without hesitation. My knees and feet were together, stiff and taut, while my arms grabbed the edge of the hole behind me. I was anxious to make a clean exit, not like my last one at Ringway. This time I had the advantage of going out with my back to the slip stream. My eyes were fixed on the Sergeant's right arm held up in the air. His thumb and forefinger formed a circle for good luck, with the three other fingers sticking straight up. Any time now. "GO!" he roared, and swung his right arm down. As I pushed off I quickly raised my right arm and returned his good-luck sign, then grabbed my pants legs and swam into the slip stream. It was broad moonlight. Spies and saboteurs go out, like cats, when the moon is high.

19 · "Hands Up!"

As YOU jump from a plane, the slip stream hits you. It is as though you had leaped to the water in the wake of a speeding battleship. In the two seconds before your chute opens you are hurled and buffeted in the rushing current of air. The static line is whipped against you. It may nip off your ear or break your nose, or twist around your neck and strangle you. Or the gale may set you spinning so fast that the chute does not have a chance to open. I once saw a British officer deliberately set himself spinning in the slip stream and then reverse his motion and spin in the opposite direction to let his canopy unfold. That was an experimental jump. Or the wind may rip a hole in the chute or blow it against the plane so that one of the risers or canopy lines is cut. If that happens, the canopy will flop wildly about, out of control. Instead of wafting you gently to earth it will dash you against the ground, drag you up and drop you down again. Your only chance of survival is to unbuckle your harness as you approach the ground and, at the last minute, let yourself fall free. Then you may escape with only a broken bone or two.

Fortunately none of these things happened to me. For a moment the stream swooshed around me, then I had dropped away and was sailing through the air. I felt the uplift of the opening shock, the tug of the shoulder and leg straps, and my canopy opened. It was a beautiful canopy, camouflaged dirty brown, and it gave the illusion of swinging to and fro. In reality it is the parachutist, not the canopy that swings. This pendulum swinging must be curbed by shortening the canopy cords, or risers. Otherwise you will strike the ground with great force and may even swing up again twenty or thirty feet and come down flat on your back. This experience will make you apprehensive about taking other jumps. One of my best friends in O.S.S., Chester Bradford, broke his back in this way on a parachute jump at Ringway. Chester belonged to an old New England family, related to a former President. He went to Harvard, but for reasons he never made clear he ran away to join the French Foreign Legion and won fame for his daring in desert campaigns among the most hardened fighters in the world. He was never drunk and rarely sober. As soon as his back was mended Chester jumped again, this time into France as one of a five-man team of saboteurs. Two of the team volunteered to try out a new type of static line made of metal. It snapped and both men were killed. Chester himself landed safely but that same day the village where they were hiding was surrounded by the Germans, who threatened to kill all the villagers unless the saboteur team gave themselves up. Chester's commanding officer walked out into the open and surrendered, giving the other two time to get away. After lying all night in a sewer with a bullet in his leg Chester escaped with the sergeant and completed his mission.

My plane roared off into the distance. Boxes, baskets and containers, each attached to a parachute, dropped past me. As I had been taught at Ringway, I held my knees and feet together, tucked in my head and clutched the risers to my chest. I hit the ground hard, crumpled up and rolled over to break the shock. Then, still lying flat on the ground I dragged off the parachute harness, pulled out the .45 Colt, and peered around over the barrel. All around me were scattered the boxes, baskets, and containers with their flapping canopies. Soon I saw figures running toward them and heard excited voices babbling in French. The lights of a truck guided them as they scrambled for the cargo. One box had exploded and there was a lot of shouting and running around it. No one came to look for me. "To hell with them," I said aloud and began rolling up my chute. Then two Frenchmen together pointed in my direction and one of them began running towards me. I put the chute under my arm and walked to meet him. About ten yards from me he stopped dead. In my best French I asked, "Comment allez-vous?" His mouth gaped, his eyes stared. Without a word he turned and ran, faster than before, to the other Frenchman. I walked after him. Side by side they advanced, each with a Sten gun aimed at me.

"Je suis Américain," I said. They did not reply. I stood still. They circled around me suspiciously. "This is a helluva way to treat an American," I said out loud. Then I tried swearing mildly in French but their only answer was to shout "Levez, levez!" and jerk their Stens upward as a sign to me to raise my hands. I hurled curses at them and smiled in the hope of provoking them. They gestured with their Stens in the direction of the truck. I walked toward its headlights and they followed close behind. I realized that they might take me for a German. My jump suit covered me from neck to ankles, and I had no visible insignia of rank or nationality.

When we reached the headquarters truck, I was led up to a French commandant, equivalent to a major. Le Commandant was leaning against the radiator of the truck with one foot crossed over the other and was smoking a cigarette. I came to attention, saluted as smartly as I could in my cumbersome suit, and announced that I was Marceau, the American. He did not return the salute or make any gesture of friendship. He kept on smoking and looking at me out of the corner of his eye. After a few moments I grew tired of standing at attention while he looked me over and I switched to parade rest, with legs apart and hands behind my back. Some of the men had finished loading their share of boxes and containers on the trucks, and wandered over to le Commandant's command post. When they saw the two of us facing each other in silence they walked around behind me and began whispering to each other.

I began to understand. Neither le Commandant nor his men had expected me. Their actions suggested that they considered me, to say the least, unwelcome. I pictured a hole in the ground and me in it with a bullet in my head. These impulsive, excitable creatures might do away with me in error. Gerard had given me a code sentence to use as a last resort, and I decided that now was the time for it.

So I repeated, "Je suis Américain. Je m'appelle Marceau," and I added, enunciating as clearly and as distinctly as I could, "Je cherche l'homme qui ne fume pas."

As quick as a flash le Commandant clicked his heels, saluted, and extended his hand. "Magnifique, magnifique," he exclaimed with joy. "I speak Eengleesh. I av studied eet eight years een school. Ze man who does not smoke ees Édouard, le commandant anglais. I know heem. You weel meet heem tomorrow. Tonight you must dreenk weeth us and meet Alex, ze great soldat anglais."

He had not been forewarned of my arrival. Édouard had sent him to this drop zone to flash signals with the truck headlights to a plane that might come over. The drop was supposed to have been at Argenton, forty kilometres northwest, but the Germans had marched into Argenton that day, and Édouard had not been able to send word to London to change the drop zone. We were at an emergency drop field near the village of Fresselines. A garrison company of soldiers was stationed permanently at Guéret, thirty kilometres away. He added jokingly that he was in a way sorry to see me arrive because now he could not cache any of the equipment. He said it was a favorite stunt among Maquis fighters to light bonfires and to flash all sorts of mixed-up dot-dash dot-dash signals to passing planes in the hope that they would drop their supplies. In this way a small Maquis leader could overnight become powerful simply by acquiring twenty tons of fighting equipment, and could declare for himself rather than be in a subordinate command. It was risky, because Germans were known to drop supplies in order to find out where the resistance groups were. When he saw me he was sure that this had happened to him and he had been tricked. He was planning to dispose of me as quickly as possible. He assumed that the supplies were booby-trapped, the Germans now knew the location of his Maquis camp, and I was somehow capable of sending radio messages back to my German commander. I had been right in surmising that he meant to dispose of me on the spot. In short, he had been as badly frightened as I.

More than thirty Frenchmen had now gathered round me and were shaking my hand, patting my back, and pushing each other out of the way to compete for my attention. Each one wanted to meet "le parachutiste Américain" who had dropped from the sky. They handed me a bottle of red wine. I gulped it thirstily, and passed my brandy flask to them in return. We toasted each other, and drank to l'Amérique, la France, and l'Angleterre, to Roosevelt, de Gaulle, and Churchill. In a mood of friendship and generosity, I gave one of them my brown chute, another my axe, and a third, my shovel.

Le Commandant dragged me away from the crowd and I stepped into his sedan. An armed guard was mounted on the front seat, a second one in the rear. First we were to meet and drink with Alex in Fresselines, and then go on to the camp. The Maquis travelled mostly at night.

On the way to Fresselines we were stopped. Three Maquis sentries jumped into the glare of our headlights, shouldered their rifles and aimed them at the windshield. Our guards leaped from the car and pointed their rifles at the sentries. It was dramatic. When the sentries had peered at us and looked into the car and received the password from le Commandant, they waved us on. Sentries had been placed on all roads leading to the emergency drop field, in order to prevent possible German interference. True, approaching Germans would shoot down sentries prancing in the road, but the shots would serve to warn the other Maquis soldiers. At Fresselines le Commandant sneaked into a house by the back door, and a few minutes later the rest of us were whispered in.

This was my first meeting with Alex. He left Pemberley before I arrived there. With his bushy hair and black eyes he looked like a robber chieftain. He shook my hand cordially and stood there while they crowded round, extolling his latest deeds and calling him a clever strategist. He shrugged his shoulders, rubbed his eyes and scratched his head and chest as if listening to an oft-told tale. Alex had recently hijacked a German train, an operation which had yielded a carload of Egyptian cigarettes and two carloads of Dubonnet wine. Another time he and two of his men attacked a group of forty-five Germans, killed twenty-two and wounded nineteen.

"It was a simple matter, but these fellows make much of it. We heard that a group of Germans on bicycles had left Guéret, travelling east. I knew the road well. The three of us set ourselves up behind some bushes on top of a cliff, overlooking a bend where the road ran steeply uphill. We knew that the Germans would have to get off their bikes to climb the hill. We watched them coming up. They were infantrymen but their rifles were strapped on their backs. They were laughing and talking, with no thought of danger. We had a basket of grenades waiting for them. When they were right underneath us on the road, we dumped the grenades on them and machine-gunned the hell out of them. It took us less than five minutes. Even if they had tried they could not have reached us. We retreated through the woods, drove away in a car that was waiting for us, and went home. We learned about the casualties from the hospital at Guéret. It was great sport." He spoke with a slight but definite French accent. "Where did you learn English?" I asked. "You speak it very well." He looked straight at me. "I am English," he replied. I have always wondered. Alex was a strange man. His parents were well-off and he did not have to work. I have told of his dubious career as a jockey and his changing sides in the Spanish War. He felt no qualms over this. Alex was a soldier of fortune. His twenty-four Commando raids he described as "pretty routine stuff." "We took soil samples of the land along the coast or captured Germans alive and brought them back for interrogation. On one mission I captured a German by tapping him on the head with a blackjack. We laid him in the boat and we were halfway back across the Channel when I discovered that he had given up the ghost. We dropped him into the Channel."

We talked and drank until half past four in the morning. "What is your *nom de guerre?*" asked Alex, as I was leaving.

"Marceau."

"Let's change it. It's the custom when you arrive. What name do you prefer?"

"I have a brother named Frank, suppose I call myself 'François?'"

"Very well," replied Alex, "you shall be called 'François'

by all of us from now on." And so I was. London might issue instructions, but here Alex was king.

Next I was taken to le Commandant's Maquis camp, where le Commandant directed the storing of the "parachutage" supplies. Of all the Maquis camps that I later visited or lived in, this was the pleasantest. "Moulin" was its name, and it lay at the bend of a large stream, La Grande Creuse, that babbled down among the rocks. The camp was named from an old flour mill, still standing but no longer in use. The old couple who owned the place had given it to the Maquis, and tended the farmland and cows and pigs which supplied the men with food. The guerrillas, poorly dressed and poorly equipped, slept on piles of straw with their packs as pillows and their weapons by their sides. At a moment's notice, if the Germans should attack, they could blow up the ammunition dump, ford the river by steppingstones, and fight the enemy from the other side. Across the Creuse was a forest impenetrable to all but those who knew its secret paths.

There was only one bed in the camp, le Commandant's. He insisted on turning it over to me despite my protests. I felt guilty but the French are generous and sensitive and I could not refuse. I went to bed exhausted but still excited. If I had not been so tired, the bed lice would have bothered me. After only three hours' sleep I was awakened and told that le Commandant was waiting to have breakfast with me. I did not bother to shave or brush my teeth, for fear of being looked upon as a sissy, but I did manage to sprinkle some DDT powder over my lice wounds. Then I dug into one of the containers which had dropped with me the night before and pulled out a .22 silencer pistol, two pounds of coffee, and all my chocolate bars. To the miller's wife went the coffee and the chocolate bars. To le Commandant went the pistol. I sat down for my first breakfast in France, at a table under a tree beside La Grande Creuse.

Le Commandant was the aristocratic type of French officer, young, handsome, always polite, and as correct as an Englishman, yet with the exuberance of a true Latin. He covered my right hand with his two, shook it as though pumping the handle of a well, then leaned forward and asked with great warmth, "Av you sleep well?"

At first I thought he was trying to kid me. Mooing cows, crowing cocks, cackling hens right in my bedroom, soldiers shouting to each other, lice burrowing into my skin. "I had dreams of shooting Germans," I said.

"Eef you weel excuse me, I weesh to say zat een ze Maquis we do not speak of 'Germans.' Zay are 'boches.' We do not respect zem. I hope you weel help me to speak Eengleesh."

"Of course," I replied.

"You weel excuse ze food. Eet ees not very good," he apologized.

If you are an epicure or squeamish, do not join a guerrilla band. The breakfast consisted of a piece of "jambon," which was a salty, hard, granular chunk of pork, and a large bowl of chicory coffee, without cream or milk but sweetened with four tablespoons of what was called sugar. I was offered wine, but I had not yet learned to drink wine at breakfast. Le Commandant had no fork. The mess corporal gave me one, still smeared with remnants of egg, but I used my parachute knife instead.

Le Commandant must have been watching me, for he said, "Een ze Maquis we do not av comforts. Ze deeshes and ze spoons are dirty because we do not av soap. Bot aftair a while you weel be so hongry zat you weel not care." He was right.

We had constant interruptions during breakfast from hornets, and from visitors, both civilians and officers. Whenever they approached le Commandant's table they would halt, after a flourish of waving arms, come to attention, click their heels, salute, and ask, "Mon Commandant, may I speak to you?" He would either engage immediately in conversation or read the notes they handed him, meanwhile paying equal attention to his food and wine. He always introduced me to the officers, never to the civilians who, he said, were engaged in "liaison" work. I learned later that a person engaged in liaison was nothing but a courier spy who carried information about the enemy from one Maquis camp to another.

A sergeant came to report that a former member of the Maquis had been found dead and naked in the woods, shot through the back.

"Shall we bury him, mon Commandant?"

"No," replied le Commandant, and turning to me he said, "We are too beezy. He was a collaborateur."

The hornets were more troublesome than the visitors. Two of them were swimming in my coffee bowl, and I wondered if it would be a breach of etiquette to ask for another bowl. A hornet fell into le Commandant's bowl too, and I watched to see what he would do. Without pausing in his conversation he scooped out the hornet with a tablespoon and went right on drinking. I did the same.

Soon after breakfast, "the man who does not smoke" appeared, Édouard, the British major, my Commanding Officer, the boss of the Creuse. He had a pipe in his mouth. Édouard was thin but muscular, about five feet eight inches tall, with the brown face of a man who spent most of his life out of doors. He was wearing an open-necked shirt and shorts. I guessed him to be in his late thirties. His manner was stern. He greeted me without a smile.

"I am glad to have you with us," he said. "We need help badly. For months I have been asking London for six men. They promise but do nothing. You'll be kept busy. I'm sorry I didn't meet you last night, but you seem to be all right."

I passed on the few instructions I had received from Gerard in London, and the parcel containing three million francs. He ripped it open, grabbed a handful of francs and stuffed them into his pocket, and then gave the parcel to Commandant Anne, his side-kick, a Frenchman.

"Aren't you going to count it, sir?" I asked.

"No," he replied. "I assume it's correct. Do you have enough?"

"One hundred thousand francs."

"Very well," he said. "If you need more, let me know. Remain here for a few days. Avoid the village. The French are given to careless talk. If you mingle with them, the whole countryside will soon know that an American has arrived, and the news will spread to the Germans. Wear civilian clothes so as not to arouse curiosity. I understand that you have been trained primarily as a Maquis instructor, but there is more important work to do. In a week at the most, I'll send you out on active assignments. In the meantime stay here, keep busy, and teach them what you think they ought to know. Do you have any questions?"

"Yes, sir. What shall I teach them?"

"Assume they know nothing. Absolutely nothing."

"Sir, what shall I call you?"

"Call me 'Édouard.' I'll let you know when I change my name."

20 · "Cheecago Gangstair"

THERE were about fifty guerrillas at Camp Moulin. A few had served in the army, but most of them were just hungry, ill-clothed country boys who had taken refuge in the woods, either to escape being sent to slave-labor camps in Germany or because they were seeking to avenge a member of their family who had been tortured or killed by the Germans. Morale was low. They obeyed orders and tried hard to learn, but they had no fighting spirit. They hated the enemy, but feared him. The greatest tribute they could pay to another soldier was, "He is not afraid of the Boches."

After Édouard had left, I held an informal class in explosives. While the men watched, I unpacked the containers of explosives and made a few remarks about their use. Some of the containers had been damaged and the contents spoiled, so we tossed all cracked grenades and dented bullets in a pile outside the barn. A yardbird soldier came along and assumed that the pile contained waste matter to be burned. Since he was in charge of the "burning detail," he piled on wrappings, straw, and paper from another pile, and touched a match to the rubbish. I saw the flames leap up, realized we were in trouble, and yelled for everybody to take cover. We had no time to run away, but we closed the barn doors and crouched low in the corners. In a few seconds we heard grenades popping and bullets spitting, and fragments were hurled in all directions. Shrapnel flew through the barn door. The blaze was less than ten feet from the door, and the barn was loaded with at least two tons of explosive plastics, incendiary bombs, grenades, and detonating cords and caps. A single spark would have wiped camp and flour mill off the face of France in one great big boom. I should have had my head examined for being so careless. Henceforth, I would follow the rule laid down by Édouard: "Assume they know nothing, absolutely nothing."

In blowing out a bridge or cutting a railroad track, only a couple of men need to know the detailed technicalities of explosives. Most of the guerrillas act as sentries or fetch and carry and dig while the specialists handle the charges. But every man ought to know how to fire a pistol, a tommy-gun, and a light machine-gun. We also fired the Piat, an English equivalent of the Bazooka. It had a shoulder-shattering kickback. The Piat was fired only by a select team. Whenever a member of this team hit the target and knocked it to pieces they would all exclaim "Ooh-la-la!" and pump the marksman's hand.

Most of the fun came when I taught them to fire the .45-calibre Colt pistol. I spent the afternoon of the first day teaching them to "blindfold" strip, assemble, and prove it, and the next morning I took them out to the range. We selected a container for a target. It had the approximate height and width of a standing man, and we chalked out the belly area. Each man was allowed six shots. The firing procedure was simple. The soldier would crouch in front of the target, about fifteen yards away, with a cocked pistol pointing to the ground just in front of his feet. I was behind him, peering over his shoulder. At my command he would rush toward the target, running at a fast tiger's crouch. When I yelled "Fire!" the soldier would let off two quick shots, "pointing" but not "aiming" at the target. As soon as these two shots were off, he would run and hide. Then he would repeat the performance, coming in from the left of the target, and, later, from the right. The French liked this show. It was packed with excitement. They were pleased with their own agility and alertness and proud of learning not to be afraid of this massive, barking pistol which was always cocked in their hands, and they enjoyed my dramatic gestures and shouts. I was teaching them what Fairbairn, the English O.S.S. instructor, had taught me.

After I had put twenty-five students through the course, one of them came out of the crowd and told me, loud enough for everyone to hear, that it would be a pleasure to watch me shoot. Would I please be so kind as to give them an actual demonstration of how it should be done so that they could watch "le maître" in action and profit from the observation? That's what I was afraid of! An instructor should never compete with his students, because there is always someone, natively gifted, who will make a monkey out of him. I told them, truthfully, that my shoulder, dislocated in my last parachute jump in England, had not completely healed, and that the muscles of my right arm were still sore. But he insisted, they all insisted. There seemed to be no way out of it. One of the farmer-soldiers shouted, "Shoot with your left."

"All right," I replied. "I will shoot with my left, but please remember that this is a demonstration and not a test of skill."

"Oui, Oui," they chorused, and they slapped their thighs with glee.

I decided to give them a good show and put on the best act I could. Until the moment that one of them had shouted, "Shoot with your left," I had forgotten that I had fired well over a thousand rounds with my left hand while my right arm was in a sling. I found that I could shoot better with my left, because I was left-eyed. Until then I had always fired a shotgun or rifle from my left shoulder, but a pistol with my right hand.

I came crouch-running into the target like a wild bull of the pampas and let off two almost simultaneous shots; then I dashed in from the left with two more; and then I whirled in from the right with the last two. They rushed to the target to examine my score. All six shots were bunched neatly within the belly area of the target. Not one of them had been able to get more than two shots in the belly area. They huddled in a circle around the target, amazed and surprised, no less than I. One of them slowly turned his head in my direction and raised his arm to point at me. All eyes followed his. I felt like one set apart. Slowly he said, "François is Cheecago Gangstair."

"Ah, oui, oui. Ah, oui," they applauded, and rushed over to pound me on the back. This was my lucky break. I was acceptable. To them I was no longer "François," I was "le Cheecago Gangstair." The rumor spread throughout the Maquis camps that the American was a killer marksman, and some of them came to believe that I *was* from Chicago and *was* a gangster.

It was all to the good.

Early in the evening of my second day at Camp Moulin, Édouard came for me. We drove to the outskirts of a village, Châtelus-Malvaleix, then sneaked through a peach orchard and entered the rear door of a large house, the home of a prosperous pharmacist, whose puny son was the leader of civilian resistance in the village.

We waited half an hour, sipping pernod absinthe, until the leaders of the resistance arrived. When they arrived Édouard outlined the strategy of the Creuse Maquis. The Allied troops, still fighting in Brittany, were going to cut across the northern part of France in an attempt to lock off all central and southern France. This very day, 15 August 1944, the U.S. 7th Army, along with French troops, had landed on the southern beaches of France between Marseille and Nice. The forty German divisions in the center and south of France would, it was assumed, be ordered north to escape the 7th Army and to attack the Allied columns streaming across France from Normandy and Brittany. Our job was to prevent the Germans from attacking the Allies in the north, or from escaping through France into Germany. The strategy was to create chaos among all

Germans garrisoned in or passing through the Creuse. We would block their escape by blowing up bridges and wrecking roads, and shoot at Germans from every conceivable ambush. We were to take no prisoners, because they would slow down our operations. The 7th Army coming up from the South could mop up the would-be prisoners.

After Édouard had outlined the general plan of Maquis resistance, which he summed up as "Tuez les Boches," ("Kill the Germans"), he introduced me to the resistance leaders. It was the finest introduction I have ever been given, though at least half of it was untrue.

"François," he announced, "is an American officer recently parachuted into the Creuse to help in the liberation of France. He is one of the most skilful saboteurs in America. He has written books on ambush warfare and on sabotage. He has given courses on sabotage at West Point, the American Military College. We are fortunate in having him with us. I would like to have him help all of you, but since he has only two hands I will assign him to work with Capitaine Claude and Lieutenant Jim. François will divide his time as he sees fit between the two companies of Claude and the two companies of Jim. He will be in charge of all strategy in these units and he is directly responsible to me. I shall not hesitate to make changes in command at his request, if the fullest co-operation is not given to him."

These men had heard of the Cheecago Gangstair incident and were ready to believe anything. But there was one thing they could not understand. They had learned from Édouard I was only a first lieutenant; and yet I was a renowned expert. After the meeting, two of them asked me for an explanation. I shrugged my shoulders. They concluded that the American army was niggardly with its promotions.

That night I slept at the home of the pharmacist. He was a man of means and culture. He had a bathtub which was not used as a storage bin, and the faucet yielded water.

In the morning, Claude, Jim, and I met to discuss plans. Claude was a big, black-haired man in his late forties with a voracious appetite, who wolfed his food as though in competition with others at table. In between meals he would hold his stomach, grimace and wince, and complain of dyspepsia. In the first World War he had served as a private, and in World War II as an artillery captain in de Gaulle's division. In civilian life he was the manager of a Parisian cabaret. He knew his way about, was self-confident, aggressive, selfish, and always ready to filch another cigarette. But he was schooled in military discipline and co-operated cordially with me. He had two companies, 275 men, of Forces Françaises de l'Intérieur. The FFI swore allegiance to de Gaulle.

Jim was a youth of twenty-five with gold-blond hair, blue eyes, and a fair skin. His family came from Alsace. He was generous, enthusiastic, and sociable. His men were not so well-disciplined as Claude's but there was more comradeship among them. Before the war he had been a teacher and frankly admitted that he was not a soldier, but he liked being praised for doing a good job. He had the same number of men as Claude, 275, but they were Francs Tireurs Partisans. The FTP took their orders from the Communists. We seldom discussed the pros and cons of the FFI and FTP.

I did not, at that time, care whether they were socialists or communists, free-thinkers or atheists. My orders from Édouard were to lead them against the Germans.

Our plan was very simple. There was no point in destroying telephone lines. Most of them were damaged anyway, or had fallen into disrepair. We wanted to keep the remaining lines working because French telephone operators would pass on to us any information that the Germans tried to transmit over the wires. Claude and Jim would be responsible for the area between Guéret in the east and Montluçon in the west, La Châtre in the north and Aubusson in the south. There was one railroad from Guéret to Montluçon, which the Germans used to transport supplies, but the tracks had recently been torn up by Alex and his men. Our only concern was to prevent repairs.

One of the main German escape routes from southern France was through Guéret to Montluçon. The Germans were using country roads and byroads to avoid ambushes, and since we did not have enough forces for a round-the-clock coverage of all these roads, we decided to blow all bridges on these roads and, with the help of the peasants, to fell trees across the roads where there were no bridges. In this way we would force the Germans to travel over the main roads from Guéret to La Châtre and Montluçon. In other words, we would force the Germans to defend themselves on terrain *we* had chosen. Their only aim was to leave; our only aim was to box them in.

We would devote the first week to blowing bridges and felling trees. The second week we would simultaneously place and train ambush teams on roads which we had thoroughly reconnoitered. It meant work night and day—hard work—and travelling hundreds of miles. Fortunately, our 550 men were scattered in eleven camps throughout the area.

Both Jim and Claude were eager to have their respective companies blow the first bridge. It was a point of honor, and I had to make a decision. So I tossed a coin, and Jim won. We decided to assemble at Jim's biggest camp, take the men and supplies we needed, and that very night blow the first bridge on a secondary road outside Guéret. Claude and his driver followed Jim's car. Jim's driver Bébé was a madman. Always driving at top speed, he would not slow up even for villages. Half a mile before coming to a village he would put his hand on the horn. Children and dogs would run for cover, and mothers would scamper out to pull their toddlers into the house. Chickens, geese, and ducks were slower to respond, and feathers often showered about the car like confetti.

21 · How to Blow a Bridge

ᒣᒣᒣᒣᒣᒣᒣᒣᒣᒣᒣᒣᒣᒣᒣᒣᒣᒣᒣᒣᒣ

BLOWING bridges is fun, although the primary object is to give you an advantage over the enemy. Our object in blowing bridges was to delay the German advance to the north. When Germans encountered blown bridges, they had to stop and repair them or else find a way around, and in either case they lost time. Meanwhile the Maquis were taking pot shots at them from behind trees and rocks and from the corners of houses and barns, just as the Americans used to shoot at British redcoats in the War of Independence.

Guerrilla fighting is the safest kind of warfare, if properly planned. Guerrillas are always on the offensive. They decide when to attack and how long the attack shall last. Although they lack firepower, they have speed, surprise, mobility. As soon as they have made an attack, they can hurry to another ambush site and fire again. The enemy begins to think that the woods and fields are full of enraged peasants hunting scalps.

In our own bridge-blowing ventures in the Creuse, our aim was not only to slow down the Germans, but also to confine them to a few routes along which we had concentrated ambushes. A German column on the march was usually guided by radio from reconnaissance planes, so that they could avoid impassable roads.

Every guerrilla leader has pipe-dreams, and I had one of my own. Here it is: There are two mountains close together separated by a deep valley. Along the side of one mountain runs a road, plainly visible from the top of that mountain and also from the opposite mountainside. There are two bridges on this road, separated by a one-mile stretch. Knowing that the enemy is coming, I place explosive charges in these two bridges. When the enemy convoy has completely filled the one-mile stretch of road, I blow the two bridges and strand the convoy. The poor fellows left on the road can either jump off the road into the deep valley below and smash themselves against the rocks, or climb the steep mountainside and be annihilated by machine-gun fire from the guerrillas at the top. If they remain on the road, the guerrillas from the opposite mountainside will be spraying them with lead and those on the mountain above the road will be hurling grenades upon them. Needless to say, my dream never came true. The Creuse is hilly and mountainous for the most part, but the important roads and bridges are on level terrain.

Anybody can become a bridge-blowing expert in a week. Even in one afternoon he can learn enough to set himself up as an expert, if he is far away from home and nobody with him knows anything about explosives. Fortunately for me the Frenchmen working with me, contrary to their own belief, knew nothing about blowing bridges, while I had had at least three days of instruction, though I had forgotten most of it. For anyone who wants to go into business for himself in this field I shall give a few simple pointers, with which experts won't agree (These remarks apply only to concrete bridges not more than one hundred and fifty feet long, with few steel girders. If you are going to blow a steel-girder bridge, you had better consult a West Point engineer.):

Be sure to bring along picks, sledge-hammers, and strong men. You dig three holes, each from three to five feet deep, one in the middle of the bridge, the other two at the ends. By the "ends" I mean a place not on the bridge itself but behind the abutment which connects the bridge with the land. Knocking out these abutments makes it harder for the enemy to repair the bridge, since he must build new supports for his beams. After you have dug these holes you are ready to place charges in them. (The word "charge," by the way, refers to the complete affair, which includes the explosive, the detonating cord, the detonating cap, and the fuse.) First you put in the explosive itself, such as ammonium nitrate which "pushes" rather than "cuts." An explosive that cuts penetrates like a bullet, whereas an explosive that pushes crumbles and shatters things. You might have to use a combination of cutting and pushing explosives, if you want to cut through a steel girder and push through concrete. After you have put in your explosive, which will weigh anywhere from twenty-five to a couple of hundred pounds, you wrap detonating cord around it and connect the different charges in the three holes with detonating cord. If you don't use this precaution of con-

HOW TO BLOW A BRIDGE 195

necting all charges with detonating cord, the charges may go off at different times, losing much of their effectiveness. For if one charge goes off first, the second and third charges may be so damaged that they will not go off at all, and even if they do, they have lost a lot of their zip and may be working against each other.

All right, you now have the explosives in the holes and you have connected the explosives with detonating cord. Then you attach two detonating caps to the cord in one of the holes, or else bury the two caps in the explosive. To each one of the caps you attach a fuse, the sort of thing you light when you are setting off firecrackers. These two strings, or fuses, must be long enough to ensure that by the time they have burned to reach the caps, you are already far away and in shelter, so you must know their speed of burning. Don't worry about the speed of burning of a detonating cap, or detonating cord, or explosive. They usually don't burn, they just blow up with a bang. The fuse burns and sets off the cap and detonating cord which in turn sets off the explosive. Now that you have placed the charges in all three holes, you fill up the holes with closely packed earth, interlarded with many heavy slabs of concrete or big rocks. Make sure you pack the holes firmly, or else the explosion will push away the packing and waste itself. This done, you pick up the two fuses which are connected with the caps in one hole. This "double initiation" means that you have practically a sure-fire thing. If one fuse should be wet, or for some other reason does not send its spitting fire to the cap, you have the other to depend upon. Now you light the fuses with a match—don't rush, take it easy. First you light one fuse. Then the other. Don't run away. Make sure it is also spitting fire. Then turn your back to these two pleasantly crackling fuses and walk away. Yes, I said *walk* away, you fool! If you run, you may trip over loose wires and ruin your set-up, or you may stumble and hurt yourself and someone will have to pick you up and waste a lot of time. They may even leave you behind if you are badly injured and they can't carry you. So you just walk away—as far as you can. When you think you have gone far enough, find a big tree and get under it, and wait for the boom to go off. When you hear that boom, hug the trunk of the tree so that the falling rocks and stones won't conk you.

If the boom doesn't go off, wait five more minutes. Then you know for sure that you have made a mistake. Now you can do one of two things. You can go home and forget the whole damn nonsense, or you can return to the bridge, dig up the charges, correct your mistake, and try again. But if you should hear a fizz while you are digging up the charges, you had better drop your shovel and take off for the trees. You may have made a second mistake.

Our first bridge-blowing was a nightmare. While Claude, Jim and I were at the pharmacist's house, we decided to tackle a bridge five miles from the town of Guéret, right under the nose of the German garrison. We studied the bridge on our maps, but they did not show enough detail. So that afternoon we drove to a point near the bridge and then crawled up close to examine its construction. It was unguarded. The three of us then drove to Jim's camp and

HOW TO BLOW A BRIDGE

sloshed through mud and mire to the stone barn which was his headquarters.

Jim told his adjutant to assemble the men. Then he introduced me and I inspected them in an informal review. Most of the men had no shoes, though a few had wooden *sabots* or clogs and their clothes were tattered and threadbare. Jim made an impassioned speech imploring them to be brave and then told them that we were going to blow a bridge near Guéret. "Are there any brave men who will volunteer?"

All of them volunteered. Every man wanted to go, including the camp cook. After many eloquent pleas and fierce arguments twenty-five men were finally chosen. Four were sent ahead with the demolitions in a small truck to reconnoiter the road and meet us at a rendezvous a couple of miles from the bridge. At ten that night Claude, Jim, and I, along with the other twenty-one men piled into three cars, one a broken-down charcoal-burning truck, another a wrecked gazogene sedan, and the third our staff Citroën with Bébé, Jim's driver, at the wheel. There was a lot of shouting and confusion.

We left the camp with French flags flying from the radiator caps and the men shouting and cheering, waving and yelling. The farmers nearby had already learned of our plans and were standing around to wish us "bonne chance." It was a patriotic mass demonstration, not a secret foray. The Citroën car was leading the caravan of three vehicles. "Why are we going first?" I asked Jim.

"Because we are the leaders. The leaders always go first." But I tried to persuade him that it was poor tactics for the leaders to go first and risk all being captured at once if we ran into a German convoy. In a well-planned expedition we would each have travelled in a different car. So he stopped the vehicles, which were all bunched together, and gathered all the men around him, though he only needed the drivers, and there was a great deal of arguing back and forth. After ten minutes we took off again. The three leaders still rode together in the Citroën, but this time the other two cars went ahead of us, about three hundred yards apart, travelling slowly, without any lights. Whenever it reached a bend, the first car was supposed to wait, survey the road ahead, and give the other cars an all-clear signal.

The French guerrillas liked to do things in grand style. There had to be fanfare. The Tricolor flew proudly on our radiator cap. On each fender sat a soldier with a shotgun, obstructing the driver's view. These fender-riders did their best to look fierce and grim, shouting "À la victoire," or "Les Américains sont arrivés," pointing to me. When they passed a girl they would ask Bébé to slow down so that they could grab at her skirts.

Finally we left the villages and entered the main highway leading to the bridge. Somewhere ahead of us in the dark the other two cars and the demolition truck were waiting for us at the rendezvous. There was no moon, and the road was further darkened by overhanging trees. I peered ahead into the obscurity but could not see more than fifteen or twenty yards. Bébé increased his speed to forty miles an hour. I tapped Jim on the shoulder and said, "Bébé is going too fast. Please ask him to slow down."

"Bébé is the best driver in all France," replied Jim. "I

have complete confidence in him," whereupon he patted Bébé on the back and Bébé nodded agreement.

The car began to swerve. Sitting in the back seat between Jim and Claude I linked arms with them to cushion the effect of any shock. The brakes screeched and I could smell the tires burning. The car seemed to be out of control. A car appeared just in front of us. Our car swerved to the right into the ditch, then leaped out of the ditch and back on to the road, just missing another car parked there, swung into the ditch on the left side of the road, then back on to the road. Suddenly it stopped. We had reached our rendezvous point. Jim patted Bébé on the back in wild exhilaration and exclaimed to me, "What did I tell you, François! Bébé is the best driver in France."

Everybody wanted to be on the bridge to help with the blowing. Nobody wanted to be on sentry duty. Jim finally persuaded some of them to act as patrols around the bridge. With us was an eighteen-year-old boy named Michel who, Jim assured me, was a demolition expert. Michel decided to dig two holes right in the middle of the bridge. I suggested three holes, one in the middle and the others behind the abutments. He said he knew what to do. When the two holes were dug, he ordered that the explosives be placed in the holes and the fuse wrapped around it, and, quite properly, that the detonating cap form the connection with the fuse and the explosive. But in each hole he was using separate fuses and caps.

"I suggest, Michel, that you place two sets of fuses and caps in one hole and then connect the other hole by means of cord so that both charges will go off at the same time."

"No," he said, "one fuse and cap for each hole is enough."

"That's not right. Besides, you should use the cord to connect the charges."

"The detonating cord is no good; I know. This afternoon I tried to burn some of it, and it wouldn't burn."

Detonating cord is an explosive. You can't burn it with a match; it requires more heat. But when it does go off it burns at about 20,000 feet per second. If he had succeeded he would have blown off his head. I tried to explain this to him, but he would not change his mind.

"I have read about all this in a book they sent me from London."

When Michel had placed the charges, Jim called all the men in from their sentry posts and told them to go down the road. Then Bébé started the car and we all climbed into it except Michel, who was going to set off the fuses. I watched him. He had fuses long enough for a five-minute delay. He grabbed one fuse and scratched it. I saw no spark, but he dropped it and went on to the second fuse. He scratched. This one sparked. He rushed madly for the car and hung on to the running board. Bébé picked up speed and raced a mile down the road. There we scrambled out and hid underneath the trees.

Three minutes passed, four, five. "It will go off any time now," said Michel. Ten minutes passed and Jim turned to me. "What do you think, François?"

"I don't think the charges will go off," I answered.

"Shall we go home?" asked Jim.

"No," I said. "Let's go back and fix the charges."

Jim's men crowded around and clamored to go back to

the bridge. It was exciting, it was dangerous. So back we went, and I examined the fuses. One fuse had ignited but had been cut through by a rock. The other had never lighted. I set up the double initiation for one hole and used detonating cord to connect the charge of that hole to the charge of the second one. It was agreed that I would count "Un, deux, trois," then Michel and I would each light a fuse simultaneously, and then we would walk to the car.

As before, Jim called in the sentries and sent them down the road. Then Bébé drove the car close to the bridge and stayed there with the motor running. The men in the car had their eyes focussed on Michel and me. "Un, deux, trois," I said. He scratched his fuse and dashed for the car. I had to scratch mine twice before it started fizzing. Then I picked up Michel's fuse; it had not been lighted. I scratched his and set it going. By this time Jim and Michel and Bébé and the two guards in the car were pleading for me to hurry along. "François, vite, vite, allons, François." Before I could shut the door, the car speeded off like a spurred horse, though we still had three minutes' grace. We were then half a mile away under the trees. The charges went off on time. A few seconds after the explosion clods of earth and small stones showered through the branches. As soon as they stopped falling everyone dashed toward the bridge, either on foot or in the cars.

"Why are we going back to the bridge?" I asked Jim.

"To see the damage."

"But there's nothing we can do about it now. We can come back quietly later to inspect it. The Germans may be on their way here already."

"My men would be unhappy if they did not see the bridge now," replied Jim.

The whole bridge span was gone. The two charges had apparently gone off simultaneously. Debris was already jamming the flow of the river and threatening to make a lake of the area. But the abutments were still standing. The men of the Maquis oohed and aahed and jumped for joy and cried, "Très magnifique." They crowded toward Michel to shake his hand. Soon we were racing away in our cars and the soldiers singing triumphantly. We stopped at a farmhouse in the mountains where a friend of Jim's had prepared a feast in honor of the first bridge. I had not seen so much food and drink since I left the States—slabs of butter, whole hams, huge round cheeses, flagons of red wine. Swarms of flies buzzed around the kitchen but no one seemed to mind.

The feasting and drinking lasted until four in the morning. On our way back to camp a frightened rabbit raced out ahead of us on the road. Bébé, egged on by Jim, switched on his headlights and gave chase. The rabbit scurried into the bushes. Bébé slowed down the car, pulled out his pistol, and fired a few rounds after it.

In the weeks that followed we blew a number of strategic bridges. Some of the guerrillas grumbled because they had been left out. So we agreed to let them blow small unimportant bridges on condition that they would encourage farmers to fell trees and block off main roads. In this way many important roads were blocked at the cost of half a dozen useless bridges. At last London sent orders that no more bridges were to be blown without their permission.

22 · Get in Place

HAVING blown all strategic bridges in our area we began to lay ambushes. Jim, Claude, and I scoured the country in our Citroën with Bébé at the wheel, in search of good ambush sites. They were not easy to find, for in many places the Germans had burned the roadside foliage and shrubbery to prevent the Maquis from laying ambushes.

I was grateful that our instructors in England had toughened our feet and legs in long marches over rough country. In surveying ambush sites, we would cover ten to twenty miles a day on foot, traversing fields, swamps, woods, and stony ground. Civilian clothes were not designed for this life. Burrs stuck to my loose trousers; brambles tore my thin shirt; my low shoes became sodden and would not dry. Édouard had told me to hide from French civilians but now it seemed that every man in the Creuse had heard of me. It was even rumored that a whole platoon of American soldiers had arrived. If I were caught by the Germans my halting French would betray me at once. They would shoot me as a spy no matter how I was dressed. Meanwhile why be cold, wet and footsore? I threw away the ragged remnants of my civilian suit and from then on wore paratroop boots, field jacket, and jump pants.

Besides strong legs it takes patience, an eye for detail, and field-glasses to choose good ambush sites. I always asked myself, "From this particular site what damage can we inflict on the Germans, and how can they retaliate?" Now we would lay an ambush behind rocks or rock piles; now at a road junction, on a curve or top of a hill, where the woods lay close to the road. We tried to avoid a consistent pattern which would give us away. A site must command a clear view of the road, yet it must not be easily seen from the road. It must be camouflaged, protected from enemy fire, and difficult of access on all sides. It must have an escape route that cannot readily be detected or followed.

On our journeys Bébé was a constant trial. I kept urging him to drive slowly, upon which he would slow down from fifty miles an hour to forty. At that speed we were whizzing past good spots. He finally became angry and for a few days refused to speak to me or offer me any wine from his bottle. When he was angry he was more apt to obey my instructions.

The ambush team always had to be trained on the job, and part of their training was psychological. The French had succumbed to the German propaganda of invincibility. The rumor was current that the Germans had developed a pill to transform water into gasoline. More than one person told me he had, with his own eyes, seen the German vehicles fill their gas tanks with water at gasoline stations. The officer in charge would then carefully drop one pill into each tank and the convoy would drive on. We derided the German claims; told our men again and again that they had all the advantages; picked team members who could work together; answered all their questions honestly; and made them rehearse their roles every day.

Each man had exact instructions—"Fire only fifty rounds from the Sten," or "Throw only three grenades," or "Shoot first at the driver and then into the body of the truck." Men on ambush must be trained to behave automatically. If they are left to think for themselves, they will lose their heads. They may attack at the wrong time, or then not attack at all, or throw away weapons and flee.

We had different types of ambush teams. The gammon grenade team was usually placed on a hill or a ledge overlooking the road. The gammon grenade is a most effective instrument of ambush warfare. The usual type of fragmentation grenade, familiar to men in the British and American forces, has a delay time of four seconds before explosion. This sometimes allows the enemy to pick it up and throw it back. For that reason, whenever we were forced to use the fragmentation grenade our men were told to count "one hundred and one, one hundred and two" and then throw it. But even when this hazardous precaution is taken, the fragmentation grenade is none too effective, unless you are throwing it in the midst of a group of men. In convoy the enemy are generally inside trucks, cars, or tanks. If you toss the fragmentation grenade against a truck, it will bounce off, fall to the road, explode, and, at best, merely burst a tire, damage the motor, or perhaps wound a few occupants of the truck. It does not cause havoc.

The gammon grenade is far more useful. It is pear-shaped and made of plastic explosive molded around a detonating cap and fuse and held there by a skirt of black cloth. You can build one any size you want. If you want to kill men as well as destroy supplies you add old spikes, nails, and bits of steel to the molded plastic. When you are ready to throw the gammon you loosen a release string and throw it, taking care not to jerk it as you throw. The gammon explodes upon contact so that the grenadier must be careful that in its flight it does not hit even the twig of a tree. When a gammon hits the side of a truck, the truck and all its occupants are done for. The gammon explodes with a great boom which ends suddenly, leaving a vacuum of noise only partly filled by the clatter of falling fragments. Of all ambushes, the gammon grenade team is the most satisfying. The results are visible, definite, and complete.

We also had rifle teams, machine-gun teams, bazooka and Piat teams, and combinations of these teams. On a particular ambush the team usually consisted of three men. There might be two grenadiers and one rifleman, or two machine gunners (operator and assistant) with a rifleman, or two men on the bazooka or Piat (one firing, one loading) and a rifleman. All three might be riflemen. There always had to be one rifleman in case the team was surprised and had to flee. He was the last man to leave, covering the retreat of the others.

I constantly had to remind the sociable French that it would do no good to have an ambush if anyone else knew about it. When bored with waiting, the men were inclined to stroll out on to the road and engage a passer-by in conversation. It was impossible for a Frenchman to believe that anyone who talked and looked like a Frenchman could be a spy. It never occurred to them that, even though a person was not a spy, he might inadvertently give away the ambush location to someone who was.

I found that in the Creuse the most suitable all-round weapon for guerrillas is the American carbine. It has an effective range of at least two hundred yards, and it is light and easy to handle. The folding-stock type, especially, is a gem, since you can fold back the stock and fire it like a pistol from the window or through the windshield of a moving car. Perhaps in the Alps, and certainly in some parts of China where ambush fighting is at longer ranges, the American M-1 rifle, the British Bren, or the American Browning Automatic Rifle would be more suitable. The British Sten, because it had a range of less than 200 yards and jammed so easily, was sometimes no more useful than a B.B. gun.

While we were placing and training our men, neighboring Maquis groups importuned us to join them in an attack on the German garrison of 300 men in Montluçon. Jim was inclined to say "yes," but Claude and I dissuaded him. The other group tried it alone. They surrounded the garrison at Montluçon with hundreds of men and ordered the Germans to surrender.

The Germans stole out of the camp and into the fields and surrounded their besiegers. Being more skilful at infantry warfare of this sort they thoroughly beat the French. Jim attended the funeral services.

In guerrilla warfare you cannot wage pitched battles

requiring large forces, well-trained, and heavily equipped. Native guerrillas are usually poorly trained in regular warfare and have only a small supply of arms and you cannot afford to lose men and equipment. We preferred to leave the Germans alone so long as they remained in their garrisoned cities, but as soon as they came out on the roads we dictated the terms of the fighting. We had the advantage of being able to see them, while they could only guess where we might be.

In the course of our ambush planning, Claude and I paid our respects at the grave of a former American spy. He was on the road with his chauffeur and his radio operator, a French girl who had been sent with him from London. As they rounded a bend at high speed, they came suddenly upon a German truck parked ahead. The chauffeur had no time to think, and instead of putting on speed and hoping to get by, he stopped and tried to turn the car. Naturally the Germans opened fire. When they arrived the chauffeur was dead and the American lying wounded by the roadside. He looked up at the Germans and said in English, "I am an American." The Germans fired fifty rounds from a submachine gun into his body, cutting it in half. The girl, unharmed, was taken prisoner and interrogated with the customary beatings and tortures. She denied any knowledge that the American was a spy, and claimed that she was merely his mistress. She was finally released.

A few days later we realized that the same thing could happen to us. One of our small trucks with two men and a chauffeur was driving to an ambush site. They were driving fast and had not looked to reconnoiter the road ahead. They, too, ran into Germans—three trucks in the bend of a road. Since the Germans' trucks completely blocked the road, our men had no choice but to jump out of their truck and hide in the woods by the roadside. The Germans opened fire. Foolishly our men returned the fire, giving away their position. One of them was killed, the chauffeur was wounded in the thigh; and our badly needed truck was set aflame. According to the chauffeur they had performed a marvellous exploit: With rifle fire they had wrecked at least two of the enemy's trucks and shot a half-dozen Germans. I felt that we had lost, not gained, since our truck was worth more to us than a hundred trucks to the Germans. But I was wrong. The survivors were no longer mere Maquis soldiers, they were warriors. They were proudly pointed out by their comrades as men who had killed the hated Boches. They had drawn blood. To my surprise, morale was heightened by the incident. It took place, ironically, not far from the grave of the spy.

Loot began to appear in the camps, and the men looked better clothed and fed. Some had German shoes and boots, and gave their wooden clodhoppers to less fortunate comrades. The pockets of others were stuffed with French francs taken from Germans. A few wore German officers' belts and watches, or smoked German pipes, although I warned the guerrillas not to dress too much like Germans. Claude's men were luckier than Jim's. They captured a large truck, two small trucks, and twenty rifles, and a variety of pistols. German grenades became common, long, wooden-handled grenades which the men wore through their belts, although they had no notion how to fire them. In violation of orders, the men took prisoners. We had nowhere to keep them and were always afraid that they might escape and reveal our hideouts to the Germans. A few of the more trusted prisoners became waiters and kitchen helpers.

Late one afternoon one of Claude's teams marched ten Russians into camp. They all claimed to have been captured at Stalingrad and impressed into service as German garrison troops, and one said he had been a captain in the Red Army. Of course they insisted that they had never killed any men of the Maquis. They were nattily dressed in clean German uniforms and fine black leather boots, and had plenty of tobacco and chocolate.

What should we do with them? In London I had heard that Red soldiers who let themselves be taken prisoners were regarded by the Russians as deserters and would be shot if they returned home. Claude was a practical man. The camp road was a muddy mire full of potholes, so he set the Russians to pave it with stones. Then he put them to work chopping firewood and lugging heavy camp equipment. They did not object to the hard labor, but they did complain when their tobacco and chocolate and boots were taken away and distributed to the lucky grab-bag winners among the guerrillas. Claude admonished them to be quiet or he would lose his patience. The stolid Russians could not understand the jovial French and became surly, but they never caused trouble. They expressed no yearning to return to Russia, but wanted to become French citizens and work on French farms.

The prisoners told us about an interesting German tactic. According to them, forty per cent of the occupation troops in France consisted of Russians, Italians, Czechs, Poles, and others who had been taken prisoner and forced to fight on the side of the Germans. The French did not know this, for the conscripted troops were never allowed to mingle with them. These troops always had a German company commander who spoke their language. When the Germans were travelling on a road where there might be Maquis ambushes, they would release a dozen of these foreign troops every few miles with orders to walk ahead through the woods as patrols. Each man was given a rifle and one day's rations. No Germans were sent out with them. The Russians believed that they had been let loose to be killed in the woods by the Maquis, so they had immediately yelled "Camarade" and surrendered to the French. The Germans knew, of course, that the foreign patrols would surrender to the first Frenchman they met. Their real purpose was to lure the Maquis into revealing their positions by firing on the patrols, or else to keep them busy taking prisoners until the convoy had passed.

23 · Ambush at Pont de la Fargo

I HAD now been ten days in the Maquis camp. The bridgeblowing was over. We had successfully ambushed a number of German trucks, but there had been no opportunity of carrying off a grand coup. Then, on August 23, at eight o'clock in the morning, the telephone rang at Jim's headquarters. He answered it and his voice rose high with excitement. Then he turned to me, his face flushed red. "Two thousand Germans are getting ready to leave this morning from Guéret to Montluçon. Mostly trucks with some light tanks." The big chance had come.

Unfortunately most of the men had already scattered for patrol or ambush duty, and only two teams had been sent out that morning to Route Nationale 145, the main highway from Guéret to Montluçon. The Germans were forced to use this highway, for we had blown bridges and felled trees on every alternate route. Halfway between Guéret and Montluçon, on Route Nationale 145, was a junction called Pont de la Fargo, with a small bridge crossing a stream. We would blow the bridge before the Germans arrived. True, London Headquarters had forbidden us to blow any more bridges, but we knew they would not complain if we brought off a successful coup. Pont de la Fargo was good ambush terrain, with a concrete house near the bridge, stone walls, trees with dense foliage. My heart beat fast, but I tried to seem calm.

"What shall we do?" asked Jim.

"Get all the men you can, and all the cars. Have the men gather up all the explosives. We'll blow the bridge and ambush the Germans at Pont de la Fargo. You and I and some of the men will go ahead, after you have given the orders. The rest can meet us there, but they must be careful when they get near the road. The Germans might have scouts out. Tell the men to hurry, and they must bring their weapons. If anything goes wrong, tell them to meet us at Beaupêche."

As Jim relayed the orders, the commotion began. It became bedlam. Lieutenants screamed at each other. Men hustled and bustled. Everyone begged to come. The cook and his helpers threw huge loaves of bread and hunks of cold meat and bottles of red wine into the trucks, grabbed rifles, and came to join the fray. This time all were welcome.

As soon as Jim and I reached Pont de la Fargo with one group of men, we stationed guards one mile from the bridge on either side. Their orders were strict. "Commandeer all the cars and trucks you can get hold of. Search every pedestrian and cyclist thoroughly. If you have the least suspicion that one of them may be a spy, hold him. No one must use this road. Tell people to find another way around. Shoot anyone who argues or puts up a fight. But if you say, 'Keep away from this road, the Germans are coming,' you won't have any trouble. Question all travellers from Guéret about the Germans. Try to find out what supplies they have and how much armament, and how they are travelling. Keep a special look out for Miliciens. The Germans may send them ahead as spies." These Miliciens, the French security police, were as dangerous as the Germans, and even more hated. As an added precaution, we also sent patrols in a half-mile radius around the bridge.

There was a small cluster of houses near the bridge. We frightened the occupants out of their homes by telling them that the Germans were on their way from Guéret, burning, pillaging, raping. Close to the bridge, on the Guéret side, a small road from Beaupêche joined Route 145. Across this road, thirty yards from the main road, we felled a tree about two feet in diameter and parked our cars a mile beyond it on the Beaupêche side. This barricade served the double purpose of screening our ambush and protecting our escape afterwards.

Four times during the morning a small German scout plane flew over the road. Each time we scuttled into hiding.

By eleven o'clock that morning we were beginning to wonder if we could be ready in time. Just before twelve Jim came to me and said, "We have a dinner engagement at noon."

"What does that matter?"

"But the other day I invited Lucille and Lorraine to have dinner at the camp with us today, in your name and mine."

"You're crazy," I answered angrily. "You had no right to

invite anyone in my name without my permission. Besides, who will manage the radio station if the girls are having dinner with us? You'll get me into trouble with Édouard."

"Won't you come to dinner?" he pleaded.

"Of course not."

"But Lucille will be disappointed."

"I don't care. This is no time to talk about dinner and girls, when the Germans are coming. Lucille will understand."

"But there will be no one at the camp to meet them."

He wanted me to tell him he could go. In this mood he was useless. Most of the morning he had stood idly by while I directed his men. There was no sense arguing with him any further so I sent him on his way.

"I shall return as quickly as I can," he said happily as Bébé drove him off.

We did not have enough explosives—no dynamite, no ammonium nitrate. All we had was a small amount of plastic explosive and eight anti-tank mines. There was no time to send to far-away camps for more explosives. We needed every man. We dug across the road on the bridge, planted the mines in the holes, molded the plastic around the mines, and connected all the charges with detonating cord. It was unsatisfactory but the best we could do.

Should we blow the bridge before the Germans arrived? Or should we let their tanks and trucks explode the mines and charges? The second idea appealed to me, but the mines might not go off, or the damage might not be great enough to stop the column. If we blew the bridge beforehand, we must do it while they were still too far off to associate the noise with the bridge. If only we had electrical detonating apparatus we could blow the bridge right in their faces!

About four o'clock Jim returned, expecting to find the whole thing over. But the Germans were slow in coming. They must be having trouble from other ambush teams. There was constant firing of mortars and artillery in the distance. They must be creeping along. The afternoon passed. No Germans. Yet Guéret was less than twenty miles away. If they had left at nine and were travelling at normal speed they should have been at Pont de la Fargo by eleven. Perhaps they had sent out flanking scouts to patrol the woods ahead. That would slow down their advance to walking speed.

At seven o'clock, as the sun was setting we blew the bridge. Rocks and stones scattered hundred of yards, but the bridge was only partially destroyed. Trucks would not be able to cross, but pedestrians and bicyclists could walk along a ledge at the side, and tanks could go down into the hole and up and out. The men worked furiously with picks and shovels to deepen and widen the hole and break down the ledge. When we had finished, even a tank would scarcely be able to cross.

Jim and I inspected the ambush positions. Some of the men were frightened by the sound of the German mortar fire.

I told them they had nothing to fear, because they had all the advantages. "How can the Germans hit you with mortar fire when they don't know where you are? You'll only be firing for a few minutes. By the time the Germans adjust their sights, you will be gone. Remember, the Boches are running out of France. This may be your last chance of killing them." Having reassured the men I gave my final orders:

"Do not open fire until you hear the burst of my Sten near the bridge. I shall fire one long and two short bursts after the convoy has halted. When you hear my signal, fire your rifles or throw your grenades into the cabins of the cars or trucks. That way you have a better chance of killing drivers and officers. We will meet at Beaupêche after the ambush."

I made them repeat these instructions to me. Then I warned them that the next day I would inspect their posts and count the empty shells to find out whether anyone had disobeyed my orders. Any man who threw away his weapon had better not return at all.

There was a little tyke of a grenadier whom I had stationed twenty feet from the road. I found him in a drainage ditch right by the roadside. His job was to toss four gammon grenades into trucks.

"I did not place you here," I said.

"This is a better place."

"You'll be well protected at the other spot. It's dangerous here."

"Yes, but here I can be accurate. I don't have so far to throw. Don't worry, Lieutenant François, I know what I'm doing. I was a soldier in the Regular Army. I have fought the Germans before." His face was one big grin. I grinned in return and agreed that he was right. He had the guts of a fighting man.

The forty-odd guerrillas were scattered along both sides

of the road over a distance of two miles on the Guéret side of the bridge. The bazooka, Piat and Bren guns each had three men; the grenadiers and riflemen were alone at their posts. Each man had an assigned field of fire. I placed Jim about three hundred yards from the bridge. At that range his Sten gun would be ineffective, but I had some doubts about his anxiety to take part in the fighting. At any rate, he made no protest at being put in the safest place. I stationed myself with a Sten gun behind a rock twenty yards from the bridge.

The night was dark and it began to drizzle. The drizzle became a wet blanket covering the earth. Nothing to do but listen, look, and wait. The boom-boom came closer. I saw the dim lights of the column top the rise of a hill two miles away. They had stopped firing into the surrounding fields and woods. Very slowly, they crawled down to the bridge. I knelt behind the rock and peered around the side. There was not much to see. They were there all right, but their headlights, covered with dark paper or cloth, let out only weak slits of light. A small tank was leading the column with a truck behind it. The tank came to the bridge and stopped. There was a delay. The tank managed to go down the culvert where the bridge had been and started up the road on the other side. The truck stopped at the culvert's edge.

Now I could hear guttural voices. Someone was giving orders. I heard people scuffling about, near the truck. Then a match was struck, and a light brought to a cigarette within cupped hands. I could see the man now, on the side of the road, facing me. While he was lighting his cigarette, another man joined him. Then the first man began to bark more orders to the second and waved in my direction. I had been training my sights on him and he was still waving and yelling as I sprayed him and his companion. They fell. Were they dead? I sprayed them after they fell, and then fired into the cabin and body of the truck. I crouched behind the rock and listened. All was silence. What? Were the Maquis going to falter? Had they already fled? It seemed that minutes were passing and there was no noise, but it must have been only two or three seconds. And then it began, the pleasant chattering sound of the Bren. My men had opened fire. And then I heard the crack of the rifles, the clatter of the Stens, the finality of the exploding gammons with their momentary flashes of light. All up and down the road the French had opened up, and it sounded as if they were arguing with one another, trying to get in the last word. Stens stuttered, rifles objected and interrupted, the Brens but-but-but-butted, while the gammons and the bazookas always concluded with exclamation marks, and settled the argument for a moment. I was proud, proud of them and pleased with myself. I reloaded my Sten and scurried to another spot, behind a large tree. I looked at my watch. The hands showed a few minutes before or after eleven, but it was too dark to see them plainly.

Now the Germans replied and drowned out our peeping squabble. They were furious. Their heavy machine guns rattled; their tracer bullets searched the forests and the trees; their mortars whoomed, their shells hissed as they heated the air. They were firing at the empty concrete house on the corner. Then they began to shoot flares to find us. Between the thundering bursts of the Germans I could hear the men of the Maquis firing back. A huge searchlight on top of a tank or truck was cast in my direction and searched the area. I stayed behind the tree and saw the light make a shadow of it. After the beam passed me, I fired at it and it went out. My area was again searched, this time with bullets and tracers and mortars. The tracer bullets made beautiful arches in the sky.

I was watching the tracers fly past the tree when I felt a sting in my right shoulder. With my left hand I groped under my shirt and felt the shoulder. It was moist. The moisture tasted like blood. I squeezed the flesh against the bone and felt a few small pieces of shrapnel. It must have been a ricochet.

I sent out a volley of shots towards the source of the tracer bullets, waited for the inevitable return fire, and then ran crouching from tree to tree until I was about two hundred yards from the road, where it was fruitless to fire with a Sten.

The ground had become soggy. I looked at my feet. They were swimming inside a pair of low-cut French civilian shoes. And all the time I thought I had on my paratroop boots! I could not remember how or when I had put on these useless shoes. I looked at my khaki trousers, dripping wet and clinging to my ankles. I began to notice the discomfort. It was raining harder. I urinated against the tree and shivered with cold. I buttoned the collar of my field jacket and shrugged my shoulders to get rid of a creeping stiffness.

The sounds had gone. The ambush was over. It was time to go. There were no more noises, no more lights. I must be careful not to step on branches or twigs. But before setting out I would listen and look. Then I would walk away back into the woods, cross the small road behind, and then detour around the German column. What was that? A curious noise. No, just the heavy rain dropping from the leaves on the ground. No, not quite. I listened again. It was a regular sucking noise like a foot being pulled out of the soggy ground. Was it a deer?

I caught my breath. No more breathing now. There he was, less than twenty feet away, a German on patrol. I could kill him. Easy shot. But that'll give me away. Half sitting, half standing against the trunk of the tree I followed him with my Sten. He was walking slowly with his head forward, placing each step with care, and constantly looking all around. Would he see me? I wanted to melt inside the tree. Was there anything on me that shone? I squinted to shut off the whites of my eyes. He passed away into the darkness and into the bushes and trees. That same foot-sucking noise again, behind me now. Squish, suck; squish, suck. They were walking the patrol in pairs. Then the noise died away. Should I move now? No, better stay here a while. I might run into others on patrol. All right to breathe now, but softly. Some time after the German patrol had passed I began to shake. My arms shook, my legs, my chest, jaw and tongue. What the hell's wrong with me? I'm not that cold. Am I nervous? Am I afraid? Why, of course not, the two Germans have gone. This is silly, shaking like a leaf. Can't stop it. I guess my mind's lost control of my body. Presently I stopped shaking. But I was terribly tired. I wanted to find a dry place and lie down. I looked at my watch. It was three o'clock. Where had I been these last three hours? The ambush only lasted about twenty minutes.

By now I could begin to think more clearly. I walked through the woods, parallel to the road but away from the convoy. It was heavy going through the mud and underbrush. The leaves shed water down the back of my neck. My rain-soaked cap collected water which dripped down my face and inside my collar. I was very cold. I looked back towards the bridge. The Germans must be repairing it. I saw something like smoke down there, but no fire. It might be only a thick haze.

There was no point in going farther into the woods. To reach Beaupêche I had to cross the road. I was now ahead of the Germans. The tank had gone back, but there might be some sentries. I slunk under the trees and along the hedgerows beside the road, and crossed in the shadows of the trees. No moon, but still there was light now. I tried to climb the wire fence into the field on the other side, but the fence swayed and the wires creaked. Even if I climbed it I would have to swim the stream. So I began walking up the road away from the Germans, keeping to the shadows.

Did you ever notice how many squeaks and creaks there are in a pair of shoes? I took mine off and hung them over my neck. I was pleased to realize, when I reached the top of the hill, that no one had shot at me. It had taken me ninety minutes to walk less than half a mile. There was a farm house on the hill. I tried the doors, but they were all locked. When I shook the rear door vigorously I was rewarded by a shower of water down my back from the roof drain. I waited underneath the eaves for a few minutes, trying to decide what to do. Then I walked behind the house and past the poultry shed. The chickens, geese, and ducks awakened and set up a squawking and cackling. I knew better than to walk close to a hen house, but I didn't much care now. I found a woodshed, kicked the door open, barricaded it from within, and wrapped myself in loose newspapers and burlap bags. I was warmer now. Against my will I fell asleep.

Two hours later I was aroused by gunfire. It sounded like a Sten. I jumped to my feet, grabbed my Sten, peered out of the door, and ran into the field alongside the road. The German vehicles were laboring up the road. Apparently some lone Maquis had fired at them and they had answered him. About thirty yards from the road, hidden only by small shrubs, I watched them come up. When a hooded truck came directly in front of me, I sent a burst into the driver's cabin. The truck swerved into the ditch by the side of the road and stopped. Almost immediately the shrubs were cut by a volley of machine gun bullets. Some were only inches from me. I ran to another bush, nearer the road. "This will fool them," I thought, "because they would expect me to run away from them." I waited for another truck to come up and again sent a burst of Sten fire into the cabin. It also swerved and ditched. Again the machine gun fired, right at me. The cut leaves were dropping all around me. I jumped behind a tree trunk. There was a hollow there, like a foxhole, and I nestled into it, but now they opened up with mortar fire. Three or four armored vehicles must be concentrating on me. I jumped up and ran into the woods, into the deep woods, where the trees were tall and thick and closely bunched.

I was desperate. My only thought now was to save my life. At any moment lead might pierce me. Who would care? Perhaps nobody would ever find my body and it would rot in this forest. Would anybody care? And what did it matter whether they cared or not? Only a man who has been hounded and hunted can tell you how utterly unimportant everything else becomes. Nothing, nobody matters, just you. I plunged deeper into the woods. Mortars could not hurt me here unless they fell directly on me. After about fifteen minutes I was well away from them, though I could still hear them firing intermittently, just as they had the day before. I had lost my bearings but I kept on walking through woods and fields, hoping to strike the main road. At ten o'clock I came out on the road right at Pont de la Fargo, the scene of the ambush. The Germans were gone. Wrecked trucks were spewed around. Blood stained the road and the trucks but I could see no bodies. The Germans must have carried away their dead. I walked the ambush stretch and counted seventeen trucks. One bus without seats had been filled with typewriters and tools. A gammon grenade had destroyed it. The typewriters were twisted and burnt black. Most of the trucks had been set aflame by the Germans before they left, but the French peasants and children were already busy salvaging what was left, especially wheels and tires.

As I entered the small dirt road leading to Beaupêche, an old French farmer asked me, "Were you with the ambush last night?" I told him that I was. He said, "It was a great battle. I heard the noise five kilometres from here. This is my house," and he pointed to the battered house at the corner. The windows were shattered, and the walls full of holes. I said I was sorry, but he replied, "Rien, rien," and smiled as we waved good-bye.

I walked on toward Beaupêche. The ambush had come off as planned, even better, and I should have felt exhilarated, but instead I was tired and sick with despondency. On the road I was met by Jim and Bébé in the Citroën. When I failed to turn up they had become anxious and were looking for me. We drove down the road a few miles, and stopped at a house which Jim had taken over for the day. Two frightened young girls fed me hot milk and hot coffee and I wolfed huge slabs of delicious French bread thick with butter. I began to feel more cheerful. Jim explained that about half the men had escaped the night before and returned safely to camp, and a few others had straggled in during the morning. Others wandered in later that day. Three men, who got lost and stayed with farmers, returned after two days. A few, like myself, had minor flesh wounds. We tried to estimate the number of Germans killed. Each man claimed at least three victims, but that would have brought the total up to a hundred and twenty or more. It seemed fair to estimate that two Germans had been killed for each vehicle destroyed, making a total of thirty-four. Not a single one of our men was killed or seriously hurt. The Germans had 2000 men, we had 40. We had no deaths, they had 34. They had us outnumbered 50 to 1 but we beat them 34 to zero. This explains why the Communists make such extensive use of guerrilla warfare.

24 · "We'll Shoot Them Ourselves"

TWO days after the ambush at Pont de la Fargo, a car drove up to Jim's camp and the chauffeur handed me a note from Édouard.

"You will proceed immediately to Clugnat with the driver who has brought this note. Claude will be waiting for you at Jannet's home with further instructions."

Since there was no indication how long the assignment would last, I took my sleeping bag, to protect me against vermin and lice, and my rucksack containing razor blades, soap, a towel, and two changes of underwear. The Maquis looked on these as luxuries. Jim seemed sorry to see me go, and urged that I return to his camps as soon as possible. He crammed my rucksack with cigarettes and a couple of bottles of Dubonnet wine. By now I drank Dubonnet as freely as most Americans drink Coca-Cola. I embraced Jim and kissed him on both cheeks as is the custom in France. He laughed in appreciation of the gesture, and returned my affection with gusto.

After an hour's drive the chauffeur dropped me in front of the home of Mark Jannet, the shoemaker and mayor of Clugnat. Across the street was Claude with a truck full of Maquis soldiers. He spoke to them and they jumped out of the truck and lined up. Then one of them, a sergeant, stepped out in front of them and called the men to attention. They presented arms. I returned the salute. Claude walked over to me and taking me gently by the arm led me into a back room in Jannet's home. His face was grave.

"Édouard has asked me to give you these instructions. Our strategy in the Creuse has been successful. The Germans are now bypassing the Creuse by travelling north through the Department of the Indre. They are joining forces at the city of Châteauroux in Indre. Édouard wants you to take a *coup de main* team and join Alex, who is already on his way to the village of Jeu in the Forest of Châteauroux. The truck outside will take you as far as Crevant. At Crevant, Colonel Louis, Director of Maquis Operations in the Indre, will see that you get to Jeu."

"Are we likely to run into Germans on the way?"

"The Germans are garrisoned at La Châtre and Ardentes. If you travel by the main roads, you are likely to run into them. Therefore, you must avoid Routes Nationales 140 and 143. I have your best routes plotted out on this map."

He sketched out the way, which lay over mountainous terrain. For the most part he had chosen fourth-class roads.

"Where do I pick up my *coup de main* team?"

"They are the men outside. There are twenty-one of them, including their leader, a sergeant-major."

"How were they selected?"

"It was difficult, François. I asked for volunteers in my companies. They all wanted to work for you, so I chose them at random to prove to them that I was fair."

Chosen at random, indeed! Why didn't they let me pick my own team? Suppose some of these men were no good? But I kept these thoughts to myself. "Very well," I said to Claude, "Is everything ready? Is everyone here? Does each man have a weapon, plenty of ammunition, grenades?"

"Everything is set. The men have been waiting for you." He led me outside and introduced me to the sergeant-major who came to stiff attention, saluted, and then shook my hand.

"It is an honor to serve you, mon lieutenant," he said ceremoniously.

He was not more than five feet two inches tall and weighed less than a hundred and thirty-five pounds, but he looked wiry and tough. He walked like a proud cock-robin and spoke with the booming voice of a man twice his size. The men jumped when he shouted. He was constantly yelling and ordering them about.

"Sergeant-major, were you in the army before you joined the Maquis?" I asked.

"Oui, mon lieutenant, the army is my career. I was a sergeant in the Regular Army before the fall of France."

"I am glad to know that," I said, "because I need a good man. I don't speak French very well, so I shall depend on you. Before we start out I want you to introduce me to each of the men and supply me with a list of their names and the things they are best fitted to do."

"Oui, mon lieutenant," and he lined them up. He knew all their names. There was another sergeant, polite and affable but lacking the sergeant-major's aggressive spirit. While I talked with this second sergeant I observed that he had no shoes but wore a pair of wooden sabots. It seemed to me that any self-respecting sergeant would have stolen a pair of shoes, if necessary. He explained that his feet were so big he had not yet been able to secure a pair. I looked again at his feet and agreed. They stretched out like skis. Besides the two sergeants there were four corporals, one of whom later insisted on becoming my bodyguard. The team had two Bren guns. To each Bren was assigned a gunner, who fired it, and an assistant, who carried the ammunition and fed it into the Bren. The gunner of one of the Brens seemed about fourteen years old and could not have weighed more than eighty-five pounds, even with a full stomach.

"How old are you?" I asked him.

"Mon lieutenant, I am seventeen, but no one believes me. They always ask me that same question."

"Have you had training in firing the Bren?"

"Yes, mon lieutenant, I have had training. I am the most expert marksman in the Maquis of Capitaine Claude." The others nodded assent, opening their eyes wide to convey to me that the little gunner was a dangerous fellow.

"Okay," I said. All the French knew what that meant. They pronounced it "Hoekay." "Okay, gunner, you look all right to me. But if you ever get tired of carrying that weapon on marches, give it to your assistant. He's bigger than you, and you're his boss."

Everybody laughed, including the gunner, but he replied, "Nobody carries my gun except me. I carry it, clean it, fire it." I later learned that this was stubbornly true. Even on forty-mile marches when he was bent double with exhaustion he refused to let anyone else carry his Bren.

After inspecting the team I told the sergeant-major that we were ready to start, and invited him to ride in the cabin with me. We had a long way to go.

I got the impression from Claude, as we shook hands, that he did not expect to see me again. "Bonne marche, François. I wish I were going with you." Jannet, the mayor, waved good-bye. A hundred others in the public square wished us good luck and wafted kisses to the men. The wives and mothers of Maquis men of Clugnat had tears in their eyes.

The charcoal-burning truck had no power. We would go zooming down the hills and try to get as far as we could on the upgrade. Just before the truck came to a stop on a hill the sergeant-major would yell, "*à derrière*," and all the occupants except the two of us would jump out of the truck and push it up the hill.

The military code, he explained, would be violated if we officers were to push. After a while the men began to puff and wheeze. I told the sergeant-major to forget the military code and we both got out and pushed with the men. He was unhappy about it but he pushed with vigor. We must have pushed that truck up fifteen hills and we were all utterly exhausted by the time we reached Crevant.

There I met an American sergeant and a French lieutenant who were "Jeds" (the 3-man O.S.S. teams sent out to gather intelligence and carry out operations behind the lines). The sergeant had broken his ankle in his jump and was still dragging his foot. The leader of the team had flown to England to beg for more supplies. The sergeant introduced me to Colonel Louis, who supplied us with a bus and driver for the next lap of the journey to Jeu.

This bus was also a charcoal-burner, worse than the truck we had just given up. Not only did we have to push it up the hills but it was continually breaking down. The driver would always follow the same procedure in repairing it. First he would fiddle with the carburetor, then he would clean out the charcoal tank to start a fresh fire. The bus would always start again. I am convinced that all it needed was a rest.

Just before midnight we arrived at Jeu. Alex's men had gone to bed, but we found Alex himself at the home of a Count. The Count, a silver-haired aristocrat like those in whiskey advertisements, introduced me to his three dignified spinster sisters. Alex told me later that I should have kissed their hands instead of shaking them.

After a few civilities and a cup of coffee, I drew Alex aside and said, "My men are starved. They haven't had a thing to eat since noon and they have been pushing charcoal-burners up a lot of hills. How about some food?"

"Haven't you brought any food with you?"

"They told us you had everything. What about the Count? Maybe his sisters can rassle up some chow for the men."

"Don't speak so loud," warned Alex. "They might hear you. They belong to the nobility, I hate to ask them."

"But, Alex, my men are hungry. You seem to know these people. Can't you tactfully suggest that they scrounge up some food? If the Germans should come barging in some day the Count might want us to give him a hand."

Alex was afraid of being thought impolite. The Count came to the rescue. Seeing us whispering urgently together he wandered over to us and said, "I do not wish to interrupt, but if there is anything I can do to help, you will call on me, won't you?"

Before Alex had a chance to be polite I broke in.

"Count," I said, "my men are hungry. They have worked hard all day, but they haven't eaten since noon. Do you know where in this village we could buy some food? All we need is some soup, bread, and wine." I knew very well that the village had closed its few doors for the night.

"Certainement, certainement," he answered joyfully, excused himself and ran away. In a few minutes he and his sisters ushered us into a shed behind his large home. The men were seated on benches and given their fill of onion soup, big French sandwiches with butter and cheese, boiled potatoes, ripe tomatoes, and all the red wine they could drink. The charming ladies and the Count waited on us at table. The men vowed that as soon as they got the lay of the land they would replenish the larder—and they did.

After we had eaten, I asked Alex where we were to sleep. "The village of Jeu," said Alex, "is divided by a road. There are about ten homes on either side of the road. Tomorrow you had better make camp on this side and my team will remain on the other, so that if Germans come we can help each other. But for tonight I suggest that you and your team sleep in the hayloft of the barn on our side of the road, right next to us. We're sleeping in the cow barn with the cows and bulls; we found some empty stalls."

I assigned four men to guard duty. The rest of us piled into the hay but could not sleep. It was too cold and we had only four blankets, so that four men had to huddle under each blanket. I gave my sleeping bag to one of them and covered myself with my field jacket, but during the night I had to get up and walk around to shake off the chill and dampness in my body. We arose at six in the morning, and washed at a well in the barnyard.

I found my number two sergeant and said, "I am appointing you mess and supply sergeant. Your job will be to see that our team gets plenty to eat. I have money. If you can't buy, borrow. If people won't lend to you, take what you need by force. We need meat, bread, butter, wine, someone to cook for us, a place to eat, a place to sleep. Make all arrangements today. By tonight every man must have his own blanket." He clopped his wooden sabots together, saluted, and said,

"Entendu." From then on the men lacked nothing.

After breakfast Alex told me what we were to do. According to Édouard's instructions, our teams should plan together but act independently. We were to scout the Forest of Châteauroux and harass the Germans there. Our territory was defined by Route Nationale 20 on the east and by Route Nationale 143 on the west. These routes met at the city of Châteauroux, which we were forbidden to enter. Within these boundaries we could do as we pleased.

We had one specific task. The French police of the city of Châteauroux had been secretly armed by the Maquis to fight the Germans. Then the police got cold feet and left the city. Colonel Louis had ordered us to find the Captain of the Châteauroux police, who was presumably hiding in the Forest, and to demand that he turn over to us the weapons and the vehicles which the Maquis had given him. We were empowered to arrest him and his men. That morning Alex and I, along with two French lieutenants and four sergeants from Alex's team, set out to find the Captain of the gendarmes.

We went through the woods, stopping to make inquiries at every shack, and about noon we found them. He tried to convince us that he and his men had been forced to flee, because the Germans had discovered their plans and were going to kill them.

"Where are the weapons?" asked Alex.

"We threw them into streams and rivers, when we left Châteauroux. We were afraid the Germans would shoot us if they caught us armed."

Alex turned to me. "Do you believe his story?"

"I don't know," I said. "It is clear that there is water in his blood."

Alex spat on the ground. "Where are the cars?"

"We left them in Châteauroux."

Alex slapped the Captain's face and shouted, "Swine!

If we find you have lied to us, we'll kill you. We ought to kill you now, but you're not worth a bullet. You and your police are under arrest. Go to Crevant immediately and report to Colonel Louis."

"Yes, mon lieutenant," meekly replied the former Captain of police.

France was full of brave men, but it had its share of cowards, collaborators, and Miliciens. Miliciens were Frenchmen who aligned themselves with the Germans, openly as soldiers or secretly as spies. Collaborators were those who willingly fed and housed the Germans and sympathized with their cause, and were rewarded with patronage and wealth in return. This weak-willed Captain was neither collaborator nor Milicien, merely a coward.

Before we left the Captain, Alex asked him, "Have you seen or heard of any Germans in the Forest?"

He answered, "I was told by one of the woodsmen whom I met this morning that a German car had stopped in Varennes."

We questioned him further but he had no more news, so we drove towards Varennes, parked the car in a copse a mile outside the village, and mounted a one-man guard on the dirt road nearby. Besides watching the car he was to protect our rear and to prevent anyone from entering the village until we had returned. Before we started out we spied a bicyclist coming from Varennes. When he was about fifteen feet from us, we jumped into the middle of the road and pointed our rifles at him. He came to a sudden dusty stop and jumped off his bicycle. He turned out to be a Croat who had worked in this Forest as a woodsman for ten years. His lean face, decorated with a bushy handlebar mustache, suggested an American villain of the Victorian period. We suspected that he might be a spy, but he volunteered the information that four Germans had stayed overnight at one of the houses in the village. We took away his French passport, to insure his compliance with our orders, and left him in custody of the guard.

The seven of us walked towards Varennes, hiding behind bushes and trees along the road and keeping at a distance from each other. We were right on the outskirts of the village when another bicyclist came down the road. He also claimed to be a Croat woodsman. Growing more suspicious, we treated him roughly and frisked him, in spite of his protests. When we showed him the passport of the first Croat he said, "He is my friend." Then he told us how, a few weeks before, German soldiers had held him up and stolen three thousand francs, all the money he owned in the world. He introduced himself as Lagic, a villager of Varennes, who wished to join our Maquis and offered to prove his loyalty by leading us right up to the four Germans in their car. Though aware that it might be a trap, we agreed to follow him.

He led us through the fields toward the road, and pointed out the car. It was apparently abandoned. We scouted the ground to make sure that there were no Germans to our rear. Then I took three men, crossed the road some distance from the car, and crept towards it. When Alex signalled with a wave of his hand, we raced for the car with our guns cocked.

As comfortably drunk as they could be, two German

corporals were asleep on the front seat and one sergeant on the back seat. The sergeant was the first to open his eyes. Automatically he reached for the pistol in his holster, but when he noticed our rifles pointing at him, he smiled and raised his hands. As they got out of the car, we frisked each man quickly, and forced him to take off his shoes. Two of our sergeants marched them off into the woods, while the rest of us searched the car.

It was loaded with loot—pistols and rifles, grenades and ammunition, blankets and clothing, and best of all, heaps of cigarettes and seven bottles of Martel cognac. I stuffed two bottles into the pockets of my field jacket. We gathered up all the loot and went back into the woods.

Alex interrogated the Germans in their own language. (He spoke fluent German, Spanish and Italian as well as perfect French and English.) They said that the car would not start because they had been given poor gasoline by a Frenchman, so they got drunk and fell asleep. We could smell the liquor on their breath, but the story did not make sense. Lagic told us that there had been four Germans, one of whom had borrowed a can and gone to look for gasoline, but the Germans insisted that there had never been more than the three of them. We made them carry the supplies we had taken from the car, except the cognac, and they walked ahead of us through the woods to our car. Two men were left behind in the ambush, to watch the German car and capture the lone German if he returned.

Alex and I discussed the problem of what to do with the Germans. Our orders were, "No prisoners." We had no safe place to keep them. If we kept them in our camps they might escape and reveal the positions of our Maquis in Jeu, but we did not have the heart to kill them in cold blood. They were obviously an advance reconnaissance party for troops coming up from Bordeaux or Poitiers, but they refused to give Alex any facts. We decided to turn them over to Colonel Louis in Crevant, who might secure useful information from them.

When we reached our car, we returned the passport to the mustached Croat and left the Germans with three guards, while the rest of us got into the car to return to the German vehicle. On our way we heard the chatter of Stens. We went ahead cautiously, and found that our two men had shot the fourth German because "He tried to fight." They stripped his body and threw him into the bushes in the woods.

We returned to camp early that evening and set up rules for the distribution of the loot. We had picked up 3400 francs from the Germans. Alex and I added 800 francs to this kitty so that each man got a hundred francs. The weapons and grenades were added to our store of supplies. A large German flag and contax camera were given to the two French lieutenants who had accompanied us. The sergeants and corporals who had helped in the capture drew lots for the watches, rings, pens, and tobacco. Shoes and clothing were given to those in need. Alex acquired a Swiss watch. I took over the German car, a huge sedan, because I had none of my own. The Martel cognac was set aside for the entertainment of important visitors. Each man in the Maquis became firmly convinced that the way to wealth lay in going out on patrol. This attitude was excellent in developing esprit de corps, but no one wanted to do guard duty.

Since it was too risky to keep the Germans in our camp, even for one night, Alex and I decided to hand them over to Colonel Louis that very evening. After supper we chose a chauffeur, and Alex and I accompanied the Germans on the long drive to Crevant. Colonel Louis thanked us, gave us a drink of wine, and we returned late to Jeu.

Early the next morning a liaison officer from Colonel Louis' headquarters came to our camp to give us various orders and pieces of information. Just before he left he casually remarked, "Oh, those three Germans. They were shot last night while trying to escape."

One of the French lieutenants of Alex's group overheard the statement and became profane. He screamed at the liaison officer, "You do not play fair. You are dishonest. After this when we take prisoners we'll shoot them ourselves."

25 · Camp Life

Men who live and fight in the bush, eat from hand to mouth, and are constantly having to run for their lives are apt to become primitive in their personal habits, especially when they cannot get the luxuries of civilized life such as soap and towels, razor blades, toothpaste, changes of underwear, scissors and toilet paper. If for even a week a man does not bathe, brush his teeth, cut his nails, wash his hair or face, shave, change his clothes, or take proper care of himself at toilet, he becomes a very smelly object. I could smell my Maquis companions three feet away. They felt that this was the proper way for a fighting man to live, and even took pride in their greasy, unkempt appearance. Like many other Americans, I too like to hunt and fish and camp and go unshaven for a week-end, and I did not want to bother the men with their unclean habits. But when we moved to Jeu I had to do something about them because we were guests of the villagers of Jeu who looked upon us as heroes, and my men were eyeing the village girls. I wanted my men to smell like soldiers and not like pigs.

Early one morning a French girl brought a couple of huge loaves of French bread into the classroom of the village school where we had our mess table. The men were seated around the long, rectangular wooden table. Her hands with the loaves in them were poised above the table. Suddenly forty hands reached up for the loaves. As one man tried to grasp a loaf, two or three others would grab the loaf and tear it away, leaving the first man with a hunk of bread in his hands. He would stuff the hunk into his mouth or pocket, and join the melee again to get more bread. Hands were bitten, shins were kicked, and faces spat at, to the accompaniment of loud curses. The men had lived too long in the woods like hunted dogs. Now that they were well-off they could not shed their beastly habits. They were human hyenas fighting over a carcass. I lost my temper. I pounded the table with my fist so hard that all the dishes and spoons rattled, and shouted, "Stop, you dirty dogs. STOP!" Astonished, they stopped. Some had soup spoons half way to their open mouths, some were still struggling with a loaf of bread, and some were drinking wine straight out of the bottle. First their faces showed amazement, then embarrassment, then fear, as I fixed my gaze upon each man in turn and said bitingly, "I thought the French people were polite and courteous. I have been told that they have the best table manners in the world. If that is so, then you are not French. There is plenty of food to eat. No man in this camp need ever go hungry or thirsty. After this you are not to sit down to table or begin to eat until I have sat down and invited you to begin. You will change your habits and eat like French soldiers and not like the pigs and dogs that you imitate. The two sergeants will sit on my left and right, and after them the four corporals. The soldiers will sit at the lower end of the table."

I called each man to me in turn. I would smell his body and his clothing, look into his wax-filled ears, rub the dirt off his face, and run my hand over his stubbly beard, if he was old enough to have one. Some were so young they had only down on their chins. Then I would say, "Your face is black and your ears are filthy. You stink like a polecat and you have neither shaved nor taken a bath for weeks. Are you a man or a beast?"

When I had finished the personal examination of each man, I said to all of them, "Each morning, at the breakfast table, I shall inspect you. If you are dirty, you will not be allowed to eat until you have cleaned yourselves. Each man must shave at least every other day. If a man is not shaved to my satisfaction at the morning inspection, I will assign him to guard duty that day."

Some of them protested that they had no soap or towels. Others said there was no place to bathe. The sergeant-major said that no one owned a razor or shaving brush. I had anticipated this objection, handed him my extra set —a razor, ten blades, a stick of shaving soap, and a brush, and told him that he was responsible for their safety.

The next day the men began to look like human beings. The local barber shop acquired some of the patrons who formerly spent all their francs at the bistro. And their fighting spirit improved along with their self-respect.

We had for camp a barnyard, owned by a French farmer of Polish descent. He made himself responsible for a German prisoner of war, a Pole, who had surrendered to us. This prisoner helped to wait on us at table, and worked for the farmer in his spare time. We slept in a hay barn, bounded on the left by a chicken coop, on the right by a pigsty, and on the rear by a cowbarn. Two guards were detailed to watch this hay barn by day and two others by night. If the Germans should attack, it was the duty of the guards to hide the weapons in the hay and warn us if we were there, or, if we were absent, to set the barn aflame so that the Germans would get none of our supplies. The farmer who had turned over his barnyard to us was not informed of these plans.

The guards were sometimes lax, and would let chickens and even pigs wander into the "barracks." I took no notice of this because the men who received visits from the pigs and chickens were loud and profane in their complaints to inattentive guards. But I often had to remind the men not to smoke in bed, when the bed was hay and the bedchamber a hayloft.

My sergeant-major was a bold and brave guerrilla fighter, always willing to risk his life, but he was an individualist. One night we were having supper about ten o'clock, after being out all day on hit-and-run manoeuvres. Lagic, the Croat, had to bicycle back to his home in Varennes that night to get messages from his friends about the Germans in the Forest. A French parachute captain, the leader of a commando team, was also at table with us exchanging information. Lagic had no weapon, and it would have been dangerous for him to go twelve miles unarmed through the woods. So I said to the sergeant-major, who always kept a clean Sten, "Sergeant-major, give your rifle to Monsieur Lagic. He will return it in the morning."

The sergeant-major replied, "This is my personal rifle. I will get him another one from the men."

"Sergeant-major," I said, "give your rifle to Monsieur Lagic."

He answered bluntly, "This is my personal rifle. I refuse."

What do you do then, if you are the leader? It was a nasty situation. The eyes of all the men were fixed on the two of us. They must have wondered, "Who will win?" The French captain looked at me in astonishment, then shifted his eyes to the sergeant-major. I knew that if I let the sergeant-major get away with this, I would no longer be able to control the men. I would, in effect, relinquish my command to the sergeant-major, and I would not be able to carry out my missions. Before the sergeant-major had a chance to take the initiative, I pulled out my .45 Colt, quickly primed it and pointed the bludgeon right at his chest.

"This is the last time I give the order. If you do not obey, I'll shoot you. GIVE YOUR RIFLE TO MONSIEUR LAGIC."

I meant every word. He gracefully handed the rifle to Lagic and said, "This is my rifle. I have been its only owner. Please treat it carefully and keep it clean just as if it was your own child." Then he turned to me and began to say, "Mon lieutenant . . ." but I cut him short with the unequivocal command, "Foute le camp." He left the room.

A few days later we received news that a lone German had spent the night in a farm house. We surrounded the house and sent in my bodyguard, a corporal who could write German, with a note for the farmer to deliver to the German. The note contained the usual warning. "The house is surrounded. You do not have a chance. If you surrender you will live as a prisoner of war. If you fight you will be shot even if you are captured alive. Come out of the house with your hands on your head." The German walked out smiling.

He told us that he was glad to surrender, because he hated the Nazis. He was the only German who ever said that to us. His wife and two children, he explained, had been killed during a bombing raid on Berlin. He was full of honey. He was a pleasant, handsome, blue-eyed man in his mid-twenties, full of poise and self-assurance. He should have been a salesman. He said that he wanted to join the Maquis so that later he could return to his sweetheart in Bordeaux. He had a collection of photographs of beautiful French girls. We frisked him, took away his weapons, set aside his bike, and then left him at Lagic's house with the sergeant-major and a corporal to watch over him until the rest returned from another patrol. I returned all his possessions except his weapons, and cautioned the sergeant-major not to talk with the prisoner until we returned.

As we approached the house on our way back the sergeant-major came out to greet us. The German was sitting on the stone porch placidly smoking a cigarette, while the sergeant-major was puffing on a big cigar. There were no cigars in the Maquis.

"Where did you get that cigar, sergeant-major?"

"Le Boche est très gentil. He gave it to me."

"Do you now accept gifts from the Boche?"

"Ah, ah, ah, ah," replied the sergeant-major, protestingly.

I looked at his waistline. "Where did you get the German belt?"

"Boche," he replied, and shrugged his shoulders and turned up his hands.

I looked at his wrist. "Is that your watch?"

"I borrowed it from the Boche."

I asked him to empty his pockets. He pulled out a handful of French francs and German marks.

He now became indignant. "The laws of the Maquis allow me to keep things from Germans whom I capture."

"Sergeant-major, as long as I am in charge of this Maquis, I'll distribute the loot fairly to all the men. Besides, what makes you say that you captured this Boche? You were only left in charge of him."

After this incident he called me aside and said he was afraid he had forfeited my trust. I told him that I respected his courage and had not lost faith in him though I sometimes questioned his judgment. He "forgave" me for publicly disgracing him.

There was another man who delighted and exasperated me. This was the corporal who, at his own insistence, became my bodyguard. He was jealous of the sergeant-major and did not like to take orders from him. Moreover, he disliked camp chores and preferred to be with officers, where he could feel important. He had great courage and was a faithful bodyguard, though he was not above snatching things that did not belong to him.

For example, one day we had taken some food from a collaborator, including fifty pounds of cooking butter and six pounds of the best spread butter. All the butter was wrapped in one-pound packages. I set aside a pound of spread butter for myself and the men who had been with me, one of whom was the corporal. The spread butter was in the rear seat, but set apart from the cooking butter. Late that night as we headed for camp, the corporal asked to ride on the back seat instead of on the fender. While he sat there, he told about meeting a beautiful young girl, the daughter of one of the farmers near Jeu. They did not keep a cow and had not tasted butter for many months. "Why not give them two pounds of the cooking butter," I suggested. "That's good butter even if it's not the best." He was effusively grateful, and fumbled about in the crowded rear seat to get the butter.

As soon as we got to our camp in Jeu he jumped out quickly, explaining that he was in a hurry to see his girl friend before she took to bed. We pulled out the supplies and each man took a pound of the "spread" butter. One man took off the paper, and smelled the butter. Cooking butter! Mine was cooking butter, too. We all had cooking butter. We carefully searched through all the cooking butter and found not a single pound of spread butter. Besides, instead of forty-eight pounds of cooking butter, we had only forty-four pounds. "Let's find the corporal," I said.

The bistro was still open, even though it was close to midnight. "Have you seen my guard-corporal?" I asked the bartender.

"Yes, mon Américain, he was here just a moment ago. He said he would come back soon." I happened to glance at one of the tables. There were the six pounds of spread butter. We waited for the corporal.

When he returned he looked at me and asked innocently, "Is something wrong?"

I pointed to the butter.

"Oh!" and he smiled with a light in his sparkling black eyes. "I made a mistake. I took too much."

"Yes, and the best butter, too."

"It was an accident, mon lieutenant."

"Was it an accident?"

He began to cry and plead, "Please forgive me, mon lieutenant François. I shall never do it again. I did wrong. I know I did wrong. I am not a thief."

What could I do with him? The men took the butter and I went to bed.

26 · Lagic

INTELLIGENCE, that is, reliable and evaluated information, is vital to the success of any military undertaking. In the Forest of Châteauroux we were so busy that I lost track of days and dates. Now that I look back I do not know how we all managed to survive the exhaustion of constant work and excitement. Although we lost touch with the calendar and the outside world, we were constantly alert for any intelligence about the Germans. We had to know where they were in the Forest so that when we left Jeu, our base, for patrols we did not waste time.

Germans seldom travelled through Jeu, because it was isolated. Only once while we were there did Germans come. Very early one morning a single German army truck with three or four soldiers in the rear passed through the village. As it went by, one of the night sentries fired at it, and the fire was returned. Both sides missed. By firing, the sentry had given away our position and for the next twenty-four hours we were ready for trouble, but nothing happened. The Germans probably thought it was a lone Frenchman taking pot shots.

As a rule, we knew where the Germans were marching, what roads they were taking, and where it was best to send our patrols and set up our ambushes. All the information came from our highly efficient espionage net. Our intelligence organization blanketed the entire Forest of Châteauroux, mile by mile. We did not pay for it except in minor services. We did not develop it, we did not train it, we did not need to motivate it, or worry about the reliability of its formation. The explanation was—Georges Lagic. Lagic, the Croatian woodsman who had led us to the German car near Varennes, became devoted to me. He did not trust the French, not even Alex, but he was attached to me, first because I was an American and second because I reciprocated his trust and was willing to follow his advice almost blindly. And Lagic was a natural intelligence agent. He was observant, perceptive, could judge people by their actions not their words, and having lived in the Forest for years he was familiar with all the roads and all the collaborators. He was the acknowledged leader and spokesman for the Croat woodsmen in the Forest. The deadly enemies of the Croat woodsmen were the Serb woodsmen. The Serbs and Croats hated each other more than they hated the Germans, and Lagic was partly moved by a desire to obtain revenge on the Serbs. He claimed that the Serbs had collaborated with the Germans in France, while the Croats had remained loyal to the Allies. I have no idea how these Serbs and Croats came to the Forest, but they had been living there for at least ten years.

As leader of the Croatian woodsmen, Lagic had almost hourly intelligence reports from all parts of the Forest.

The moment a Croatian woodsman spotted Germans, he would hasten to relay the information to Lagic either through the grapevine or by riding over himself on his bicycle. Lagic at once passed the news to me. We made use of the information ourselves and passed it on through liaison agents to Colonel Louis at Crevant, through him to other parts of France and to London. Lagic's house was our intelligence headquarters, as well as an advanced base of operations. There we assembled before and after patrols, there we left our cars and bicycles; his barn stored our prisoners during the night. We ate and sometimes slept there. Various Croats at his home helped Lagic in his work, and a small, paralytic girl of eighteen prepared food for us and poured our drinks. At first Lagic refused to be paid for his services, but he was soon obliged to accept money from me, since he could not keep this staff house operating without funds.

One morning Lagic reported that a Croat woodsman had seen some Châteauroux policemen drive two cars into the woods and reappear without them. The woodsman led us to the path taken by the police and we discovered two sedans carefully camouflaged and hidden underneath low scrubby trees. We towed them away and put them into use. It was plain now that the Captain of Police had lied to us.

We had only two or three bicycles, and since we lacked materials for repair we were lucky if even one was fit to ride. Yet bicycles were very important in the woods where cars were scarce and "essence" (gasoline, alcohol, or any combination of the two) more precious than blood. One day, Lagic reported that some bicycles had been given to a Serb who had frequently fed and entertained Germans. We went to the man's house and found him in the garage, repairing a bicycle. There were five other bicycles in the garage, and a motorbike hidden under some firewood. The Serb was a fat, gruff man in his late forties. He glanced up at the Maquis soldiers and went back to his work.

"Are you the owner of this bicycle?" I asked.

"Yes, I am, and what difference does it make to you?" he answered, and kept working away.

"How many do you own, Monsieur?" I asked.

"Only the one which I am repairing," he replied.

"To whom do the others belong?"

"To friends who left them with me for safe keeping. I don't know their names."

I examined the others, including the motorbike. Each one was either of German make or had German military markings. I spoke to Lagic and to the others, "Put these five and the motorbike into the truck."

Monsieur dropped his tools and straightened up. "One of those bicycles belongs to my wife, another to my daughter. You must take only two."

"These are all German bicycles," I replied. "I should arrest you for dealing with the enemy and not reporting military property in your possession."

He began to scream. His wife and daughter came running in and joined his cries of "Maquis bandits." But we took the bicycles.

We were also short of dishes. There lived in the Forest a Frenchman who owned a château and had collaborated with the Germans. While they occupied the Forest he profited from trading with them and had them eat and sleep in his château. When they left he boarded up his home and moved after them to Châteauroux.

We broke into his home and took the dishes we needed. I left a signed note on the table saying that his dishes, and some automobile parts and tools had been taken by me. One day he sent an emissary to see me at Lagic's home with the request that I should return the dishes, parts and tools I had stolen. I told him to send his master. The owner himself visited me the next day with an itemized list of the things taken. While I was scanning the list, Lagic mentioned that the man had a nicely painted, half-ton, charcoal-burning truck, parked around the corner. We went to take a look at it.

"Does this truck belong to you, Monsieur?" I asked.

"Yes," he replied, already sensing that he had made a mistake in coming to Varennes.

"Do you have a license to drive this truck, Monsieur?"

"No, I have no license," he answered.

"Monsieur, you should not violate the laws of France. Do you live in Châteauroux now?"

"Yes, mon lieutenant," he replied.

"Are the Germans still in Châteauroux, Monsieur?"

"Yes, mon lieutenant, the Germans are still in Châteauroux."

"Why is it then, Monsieur, when the Germans take food away from the starving and steal from the poor that they have not taken away from you this very good truck?"

"That I cannot understand, mon lieutenant. Perhaps they have overlooked it," he replied.

"I shall not overlook it, Monsieur. Does it drive well? Please get in and demonstrate how it is started."

He followed my instructions. If he had tried to drive off he would have been shot. When he finished with the demonstration, I added the truck to his itemized list, showed him my credentials from Generals Eisenhower and Koenig, and signed the list to serve him as a receipt.

One afternoon Lagic appeared with his mustached friend whom I called Handlebar Hank. "A company of Italian troops with the Germans in Châteauroux wishes to surrender," said Lagic, "and I have brought along my friend, who speaks Italian, so that we can arrange surrender terms with them."

"I am sorry," I said, "but we're not taking prisoners. Besides, what would we do with all those Italians? Where would we put them? How do we know that it isn't a trap?"

Lagic was stubborn. He believed they were sincere. They refused to surrender to the French but would surrender to an American or British officer. He, Lagic, would take all the risks and make the rendezvous arrangements. So I agreed to go with them. After all, the Italians were now allies again. We first bicycled, then walked, then crept to a point close to the fringe of the German garrison. We were met by a warrant officer, who was in charge of the Italian company, and two of his men. Through Handlebar Hank, he told me that his men found it intolerable to live with the Germans any more, ever since Italy surrendered. The Germans kept calling them cowards. He wanted to surrender all his men. To confirm his words he gave me his own pistol. But the men who were with him were not quite so eager to surrender. Would they be shot by the French? Could they go back to their garrison and get their supplies? While they were talking the Italians raised their voices and Germans from the nearby barracks began firing in our direction. I did not want to linger there, so I told them that I would give them till eleven that night to meet me at a designated spot. Only the warrant officer and six of his men appeared that night at the rendezvous. The Germans had discovered that something was wrong and set up a guard around their camp.

Before we started out, each one of the Italians came up to me and grasped my hand. Each one asked, "La parole?" I took this to mean that I would be true to my word that they would not be shot, and nodded. After we had gone about three hundred yards, I frisked each man and took away their knives, and then had them set their rifles and ammunition belts down on the road. When this was done I had them walk away, about fifteen yards, and whistled, whereupon six tired Maquis men, who had been hiding behind a haystack for hours came running out, encircled the Italians, and picked up the weapons and ammunition. The Italians were dismayed. They shrugged their arms and shoulders and kept asking me, "La parole? La parole?" We put them in Lagic's barn for the night. They could not have slept much, because the Maquis men were discussing whether they should be shot or hanged.

I had great trouble preventing the guerrillas from shooting them. Time and again the men of the Maquis told me that they hated the Italians more than they hated the Germans, because the Italians had betrayed them when their backs were against the wall. The Italians themselves didn't help. With one exception they refused to work as energetically as the other prisoners. Also, they wanted me to send them back to their barracks in Châteauroux to dig out the tobacco and soap which they had hidden. When we examined the equipment that the Germans had given them, we found that the rifles were rusty with age and lacked essential parts and the bullets did not fit them.

Next day I thankfully sent the Italians to Colonel Louis at Crevant.

One afternoon Lagic came bicycling over to tell us that an East Indian, dressed in German uniform, had been seen begging food in a near-by village. The sergeant-major, always eager for action, took off on his bicycle alongside Lagic. Forty-five minutes later they returned. Lagic had a German rucksack and rifle strapped on the back of his bicycle and the sergeant-major had the Indian on the handlebars.

I talked with the Indian, who spoke a few words of English, but I couldn't make any sense of them. He protested that he was a feeble old man and could not walk any more, but we loaded him with his own rucksack and compelled him to walk back to camp. The men wanted to shoot him and leave him in the woods, because he kept moaning and groaning.

In camp I turned him over to Alex, but even Alex could make nothing of him. Then Alex told me of a recent incident in Ardentes. Some fifty Indians had come running into the village with hands upraised, professing to have escaped from the Germans and to be friends of the French. Would the French please feed them? The French fed them and took them into their homes. That night a company of German soldiers appeared in the town and the Indians went out to meet them. Too late the French realized that they had been betrayed by these Indians, who had joined the Germans out of their hatred for the British. The Germans had used them as decoys to uncover the French who were working against them. The Indians were rewarded by being permitted to rape the women from the households that had entertained them. The Germans and the Indians then left the town together.

"He is probably one of those Indians," said Alex, "but he has lost his way. I suggest that tomorrow we drive over to Ardentes, assemble the citizens, and shoot him in the public square." No one objected.

We were going through the papers from the Indian's pockets when Alex said, "Look here," and held up a small booklet. "This is given to Indian troops of the British Army." In the booklet the Indian's name was recorded with the date of his entrance into the service, and when he had been paid. Then we found another booklet, issued by the Germans, showing that he had been a prisoner of war in Germany. We finally pieced the story together. He was a member of a Gurkha regiment, fought with the British in North Africa and was captured and sent to Italy as a prisoner of war, but escaped to fight again with the British. He was recaptured, sent to Germany, and then later into France in a labor battalion.

"My God," exclaimed Alex, "and to think that we might have murdered in cold blood a member of His Majesty's Forces!" Alex adopted the Gurkha and took him along on ambushes. He was a feeding problem. He would not eat meat nor drink milk and would take only vegetable soup. He never touched wine. He lived on bread and fruits. But he was an expert rifleman, better than anyone in either of our camps and was so well versed in the British manual of arms that we used him as the official guard to receive visiting field grade officers. On these ceremonial occasions he delighted in wearing a green turban made from a cargo parachute.

27 · "Lift Up Their Skirts"

ONE AFTERNOON, while we were out on patrol, a Lagic henchman came up to tell me that three German officers were having dinner at a farmhouse in the little village of La Maréchale, eight miles away.

"Will you go and get them?" he asked.

"My sergeant-major is leading a patrol through that area. He has probably picked up the Germans already."

At the end of the day we returned to Lagic's home. An hour later he and his men straggled in empty-handed.

"Why did you not go through La Maréchale?"

"But we did, mon lieutenant. You can ask the men."

"What did you see there?"

"Nothing, nothing at all, except a Red Cross car."

"And the Red Cross car?"

"I talked with the driver. He was a Frenchman from Châteauroux and had come to La Maréchale to seek gasoline, but did not find any. I asked about Germans and he said that he had seen none, but that Châteauroux was still full of them."

"That chauffeur was a Milicien," I said.

"No, no, no, no, mon lieutenant, he spoke French very well. I can tell a Milicien when I see one. This man was sympathetic to the Maquis." The Sergeant-major spoke with conviction.

"Did you go into the house?" I asked.

"No, lieutenant François."

"Sergeant-major, let me tell you that three German officers were having dinner in that house."

"Mon Dieu! I am sorry, mon lieutenant. But how do you know so much?" I twisted my thumb in the direction of Lagic's henchman who was by my side.

"After this," I said, "don't measure the patriotism of a Frenchman by what he says and how he speaks your language. If you had thought carefully, you would have realized that the chauffeur was lying to you. The Red Cross in Châteauroux gets gasoline from the Germans. Why should the Red Cross come to La Maréchale where there is not even a single store? Germans are crafty. They will use any trick to prevent capture by the French. I hear they are even dressing like nuns."

Early the next morning as the sergeant-major and his men were leaving on patrol, I called out to him jokingly, "Remember, lift up their skirts."

About five hours later he and his team came marching back into Jeu. The sergeant-major was walking ahead of the men with his chest stuck out. Two of his men were pushing bicycles. The others were pointing rifles at two dejected, middle-aged creatures walking with their hands clasped above their heads.

The sergeant-major approached and saluted. "These two

men speak French perfectly but they have valises filled with German uniforms." I asked him to tell me the story.

"We decided to stop all persons on the main road and examine their credentials. These two, who looked like Frenchmen, came along on bicycles. Their papers were in order, but just before I was about to let them go I remembered what you had said about believing no one. So I opened one of their valises which was strapped on the back of a bicycle. To my surprise I saw a German pistol and a German uniform. I placed both of them under arrest."

While one man was chasing a noisy setting hen out of the stone barn so that we could use it as a prison, I stepped up to the older of the two, ran my hands rapidly over his body to feel for knife or gun bulges, and then said, "I want you to undress completely. Take off all your clothes and drop them in a pile in that corner."

His eyes flashed scorn. "What is your rank?" he snapped.

"I am a lieutenant in the American army, but what is that to you?"

He stiffened up, clicked his heels, threw up his right arm "HEIL HITLER!" he exclaimed. After this dramatic performance he said to me, "I am a captain in the German army and this is my sergeant. I insist on being treated as a prisoner of war. I refuse to be examined by anyone who is not at least a captain."

I slapped his face. "From now on, captain, remember two things. The 'Heil Hitler' salute is verboten, and a prisoner's rank doesn't mean a thing in the Maquis."

After they had taken off their clothes I searched the pockets and set the contents aside. The captain had a batch of letters that he said were love letters from his wife, but they were not all in the same handwriting. He asked me to return them to him. I told him that I might return them after they had been thoroughly examined.

When the two of them had dressed again, I asked the sergeant-major to frisk them once again in case I had overlooked anything. Fingering the inside pocket of the captain's coat, he drew out a packet of letters which he handed to me. They were the same letters I had just taken away from the captain. "How did you get these?" I asked in bewilderment.

A Maquis soldier who was supposed to be helping us spoke up, "I gave them to him. They are love letters from his wife. He has a right to keep them."

I collected all their possessions, including the letters and the two valises, and took them into the Polish farmer's house to examine them more closely. Each valise contained a uniform and a pistol. In the captain's was the Iron Cross with a personal letter from Hitler himself. Various letters indicated that both prisoners had many French friends in Bordeaux. I returned to question them separately.

The sergeant pretended to be stupid. His knowledge of French had suddenly evaporated. The captain asserted that he had been the Commanding Officer of a prisoner-of-war camp in Bordeaux, and had often helped the Maquis. While retreating to Germany their column was attacked by the Allied air forces. He and his sergeant lost touch with their unit, put on civilian clothes which they carried with them, and were trying to reach Châteauroux to join another German column.

I sent a message to Édouard and he arrived the next day wearing civilian clothes. When he entered the barn the German captain turned his back on him at first, then turned round, looked at Édouard and in perfect French asked arrogantly, "Pardon me, monsieur, but are you an officer?"

Édouard replied, "I am a major in the British army."

The captain clicked his heels, and again gave the "Heil Hitler" salute. Édouard slapped his face.

After interrogating the Germans and examining their belongings Édouard said to me, "These letters prove that the captain is someone important. He admits that for seven years before the war he worked in Bordeaux, as an exporter of wine. I believe he is an intelligence officer."

He took the prisoners away with him to Guéret. A week later I learned that the Deuxième Bureau, the French military intelligence, had established that the two were spies who had helped in the internal collapse of France. The sergeant was shot, the captain hanged.

I had always thought that German spies were well-trained, but these spies were stupid or else they would never have been picked up by my naïve sergeant-major. With their civilian clothes, their knowledge of French, and their "proper" French credentials, they could have escaped easily, but they were vain enough of their uniform and pistols to pack them in the valises they carried. Even the French can be taught not to trust everyone who speaks their language.

During the last week of August and the first two weeks of September the Germans were streaming through Châteauroux. It was a junction from which they had expected to advance north against the Allied line, but the Allies travelled too fast across northern France, so the city became merely the beginning of an escape corridor through France to Germany. Châteauroux was held by a strong garrison, with anti-aircraft artillery. The Germans in Châteauroux came for the most part from the southwest and west of France, from Poitiers, Angoulême, Bordeaux, and La Rochelle. The Allied invasion of the south of France was on the tail of the retreating Germans.

A force of eighteen French commandos, as tough a group as I have ever seen, joined us in the Forest, after carrying out a daring operation. The lieutenant in charge of the group told me the story. Their target was a small detachment of S.S. troops, almost all officers, on a large estate near Clermont-Ferrand. The commandos secured a plan of the house and studied the movements of the sentry for several days. They attacked at dinner time when most of the officers were on the first floor. Two commandos knifed the sentry. Then they surrounded the house, every man hiding beneath a different first-floor window. At a signal from the leader each man sent a fragmentation grenade smashing through the window into the room. As soon as the grenade exploded, they tossed in another. As soon as the second grenade went off, they poked tommy guns into the windows and shot any Germans still alive.

The plan went off so smoothly because it had been carefully thought out beforehand. The French commandos had been trained in British schools.

We were always playing hide-and-seek in the Forest,

and could rarely find out how effective our ambushes had been. Sometimes Lagic's men would investigate our results by talking with French farmers or woodsmen and examining wrecked vehicles. In spite of pressure from my men I would not return at once to the scene of an ambush. There was always the chance that a living German would be waiting for his last shot, or that Germans coming from behind would ambush the ambushers.

The thousands of Germans entering Châteauroux appalled us. We asked London to send out planes against the troops who cluttered and jammed the roads, but no planes came.

One clear September morning I lay with my team in ambush in a thick copse at the junction of five small roads half a mile from the main road on which the Germans were marching. Three P-47's came tearing across the sky. They peeled off one by one, to make firing passes at the German columns. Their dives were followed by explosions; they must have been releasing small bombs. They made passes again and again. It was a marvellous spectacle, and brought tears to the eyes of some of the men. We longed to yell and wave to them but we kept quiet and tense, for we felt that sooner or later some of the Germans on that road would seek shelter in the woods. On one corner the sergeant-major had five men and a Bren; on the other corner, I had six men and a Bren. Between us we could cover the road junction.

The P-47's came over less frequently. The morning passed. During the afternoon the planes left and did not return. The sun began to sink and our hearts sank with it.

It was after seven and the sun had set but there was still some light. I had recalled the sergeant-major and his team to my side, so that we could prepare to return to camp. He pointed to the crest of a small hill on one of the roads. He said he had seen two men appear and disappear. I trained my field-glasses on the spot. I saw a man arise suddenly from the ditch by the side of the road, run crouching a dozen yards and throw himself down again. He was followed by another man from the other side of the road. Then a few others quickly followed them, and just as quickly hid. They had been silhouetted against the sky as they came over the crest. They might be Germans. They might also be French Maquis. We would wait.

The sergeant-major with one of his men crept across the road and placed his Bren behind a concrete slab that formed part of the road sewer. My gallant little machine-gunner, who would never let anyone carry his weapon, crawled down on our side of the road, into the sewer. He and his assistant submerged themselves in the slime with their Bren in place. I gathered the other men closer to the corner and told each man to stand behind a tree. To each I assigned a sector of fire. One of Lagic's Croat friends was on my left with a Sten. I had a Sten. I told the men, "After I open fire, you fire too. The Brens will fire up and down the ditch line. When I shout, 'Allons,' cease firing and retreat through the woods in single file; don't bunch, but don't lose sight of the man in front of you."

I peered through the field-glasses again. The men came up cautiously at irregular intervals, ran at a crouch, and always hid in the ditches. There were about fifteen of them. They followed the signals of the two men in front. They could not be Maquis—they were too well disciplined. They must be infantry men, trained to crouch and take cover. They wore grayish-green uniforms. They looked like Germans to me. I asked my bodyguard to look through the field-glasses. He looked for a second and cried, "Boches, Boches!"

I told him to pass along the signal, "Attention, attention pour tirer," and decided that next time the leading man on the right got up to run, I would fix my sights on him and would fire when the others behind him had risen to follow. They were now about two hundred feet away.

I saw a movement in the grass around the leader; then I saw him crouch low and begin to run. I followed him with the Sten. The men got up behind him. They were all running when I sent a burst aimed at the leading man. He stiffened up as though he were going to fall backwards, but instead fell face down and was hidden by the grass. Meanwhile my men had opened fire. Dust and dirt spouted all about the Germans, who were either being hit or throwing themselves flat for cover. "Tirez, tirez!" I shouted, imploring the men not to cease fire, even though they could no longer see anyone standing. The Brens refired up and down the line where the Germans had just been standing and running. The Germans had not fired a shot. Then I shouted, "Allons! Allons!" Our men scrambled back into the Forest. As usual they stuck together like sheep rather than spreading out thinly like soldiers. The sergeant-major and his assistant scurried back with their Brens from the other side of the road and pushed forward to head the retreat. I took up the rear. I was still giving retreat orders when I saw the Croat hand his Sten to my corporal and run away from the rest of us. He was running into the deep woods. The corporal now had two Stens tucked under his right arm. "Why?" I asked him, as I nodded to the disappearing Croat. He smiled and said, "He shakes." I remembered how I had been seized with shaking at Pont de la Fargo. Suddenly the corporal grabbed my arm and pointed to the spot where we had been shooting. "Let's go get their shoes," he said.

28 · A Communist and a Viscount

I WAS at Lagic's home in Varennes when one of his couriers, a Frenchman, came to say that his brother had fed and housed four Germans that night. We jumped on bicycles and pedaled for the farm. The road to Châteauroux was littered with the charred wrecks of German trucks and carts and the carcasses of horses, testimony to the effectiveness of the Maquis and the P-47's. When we arrived I sent in the Frenchman with the usual message, "Surrender and live. Fight and die." The Frenchman and his brother came out in a few minutes to say that the Germans had gone. According to them, all Germans were leaving Châteauroux that day. They had left behind them a Simca Staff car daubed with brown and yellow camouflage paint. We changed a flat tire on the Simca, pushed it to get it started, and headed for Châteauroux to see what was happening. As we approached the city we questioned peasants and travellers. They all gave us the same answer. The Germans had left Châteauroux that very morning.

We entered the city about ten in the morning to find the streets deserted and the windows of homes and offices barred and shuttered. At the sight of our German car, mothers grabbed their children and pulled them indoors. We finally found the offices of the city government. One of the men lolling outside introduced himself to us as a lieutenant of the gendarmes in Châteauroux. He said that he had fought the Germans by subversive means within the city, but did not go into details. After my previous experience with a lying gendarme, I hesitated to trust this one.

When I told him I was an American he introduced me with wild exclamations of joy to his friends, then rushed shouting across the street, dragging me with him, and insisted that we go into a local bistro to drink a glass of wine with him. In a few minutes there was a crowd outside. Women with tears in their eyes rushed into the bistro and embraced me. Children came up to offer us gifts of candies and flowers. When we came out, the crowd threw more bouquets of flowers at us, draped an American flag over the top of our car and tied a French flag to our radiator. One old woman came close to me and said that younger women had approached me and been kissed, but of course I would not kiss her. So I planted two kisses on her cheeks and one on her lips, and a great shout came up from the crowd.

I decided to go back into the woods to get our men so that they could enjoy the luxuries of an open city. At this point the lieutenant asked if I would be so kind as to drive him north seventeen kilometres to get a Maquis major who was to become the military mayor of Châteauroux. I knew that in France the rulers were the ones who got there first. This Maquis major was an FTP, or Communist. If the FTP got into a city first, they would take control and not permit the FFI, or Gaullists, to come into the city boundaries except by special permit. I told the lieutenant I had no intention of turning Châteauroux over to anybody. I had many men in the woods and we would take control.

"But why?" he asked. "I shall see to it that you get anything you desire."

"Okay," I answered, "if you give me your word of honor that you will provide me with two thousand litres of gasoline, some oil, and tobacco and cigarettes for two hundred men, I'll drive you to the major."

"Of course, of course."

We took the route that the Germans had used only a few hours before, as we headed north to tell the Communist major that they had left. The road, as before, was strewn with dead horses and demolished trucks. On the way the lieutenant, who insisted on riding on the top of the car like a conquering hero, attracted attention by firing his pistol and shouting, "Américain, Américain, Officier Américain. Vive La France!"

We found it hard to persuade the mayor-designate that there were no more Germans in Châteauroux. He was not anxious to risk his neck. But he finally agreed to come into the city. He also confirmed the lieutenant's promise that we would get gasoline, oil, and tobacco. I left the lieutenant and the mayor at the camp, and rushed back to Jeu to tell Alex. I promised him that if he would lend me his big truck for transporting the gas, I would split everything fifty-fifty with him, since he had always helped me in the past. Then we discovered that even his big truck could not hold two thousand litres of gas. He knew a French lieutenant, a Viscount, some miles away, who also had a big truck. We would have to give him a share of the gas, but it was the only way out. We had to hurry.

As soon as we arrived in Châteauroux that evening we rushed up the steps of the city hall. I spotted the lieutenant of the gendarmes in the corridor and greeted him, but he ignored me and walked away. A guard tried to block our way into the mayor's office, but we pushed past him, and lined up in front of the mayor's desk. Alex and his friend the Viscount, my corporal and sergeant-major, and Lagic were with me. I asked the mayor for the gas, oil, and tobacco he had promised. He put his thumb nail behind his upper teeth and snapped the nail forward. In the language of French gestures it means just what he said, "Not a drop." He had double-crossed me. I showed him the letter from Generals Eisenhower and Koenig which stated that the French had to provide me with food, supplies, transportation, and anything else I asked for. "But there is no gasoline," he protested and turned away to answer the telephone. The men behind me nudged me on. I decided to be tough. There was no one in the room except ourselves, the mayor, and another Communist major talking on another telephone. Lagic quietly closed the door and pushed me forward. We all drew our pistols.

"Put down those phones." I ordered. The other major dropped his telephone with a start, but the "mayor" kept on talking with his back to me. I grabbed him by the shoulder and whirled him around. "You're looking me right in the eye," I said, "and you're telling me that you don't have the gasoline you promised me this morning. I know that's not the truth. My men, and the other Maquis men in the Forest of Châteauroux, have walked twenty-five or more kilometres each day, often without anything but wooden shoes, to fight the Germans. We've gone without tobacco and without good food. We can get the food now, but you have the tobacco and the gasoline. I have a paper authorized by General Eisenhower and signed by your own French General Koenig, but you refuse to honor their orders. I want three hundred and fifty packs of cigarettes and tobacco and at least two thousand litres of gasoline and some oil. If you tell me again that you don't have the gasoline, I'll tell you that I found out today there are twenty thousand litres at the airport. We have plenty of dynamite. If you don't give me a legal permit for the gasoline, we'll get the gasoline anyway and blow up the rest of it so you don't get any for yourself. After that I'll march my two hundred men into the city to see who is going to be boss."

In a second his manner changed. "Of course, of course," he replied beaming, "there has been a misunderstanding. You will get all you ask." He signed the requisition and shook our hands and insisted on pouring each of us a glass of wine. "There must be no hard feelings."

We went to a near-by warehouse and loaded up with cigarettes and tobacco, more than enough to supply two hundred men, let alone the forty odd that Alex and I really had. Then we drove to the airport and got the allotment of a thousand litres of good gas and a thousand litres of gasoline mixed with alcohol. In spite of the complaints of airport guards, I ordered the men to put another thousand litres of good gas on the truck, so that we had three thousand litres in all.

We arrived at Jeu at three in the morning. There we dropped off fourteen hundred litres of good gas for Alex and me. The men, including the Viscount, helped to hide it in a corner of the barnyard underneath leaves and branches. We gave the Viscount six hundred litres of good gas for himself and plenty of tobacco, in return for the use of his truck. Alex and I told him that as soon as he had dropped off his gas at his camp, he was to continue to deliver the thousand litres of mixed gas to Édouard. We all agreed that Édouard should be let in on the loot, but we preferred not to give him any of the good gas. In the past, we had always turned over to him all the gasoline we scrounged up. But in return he never allotted us more than fifty litres at a time, so that we had to walk or bicycle when our fuel ran out. He insisted he himself needed most of the gas.

As soon as the Viscount had left and the others who had been with us had taken off for bed, I asked Alex, "Do you trust the Viscount?"

"I don't know him well enough to say. Some people say that before he joined the Maquis he collaborated with the Germans," replied Alex.

We decided to take precautions. The Viscount might steal our gas or inadvertently tell someone about it, who would hijack it. Gas was precious, very precious. So Alex and I spent another hour stowing away the gas in different places and covering up our tracks. We did not get to bed until after five o'clock.

On the afternoon of that day Édouard appeared. He was in a petulant mood. "Did you get the gasoline?" asked Alex.

"Yes, I got some, but not all of it. I want the good gasoline," and he went straight for the place where we had previously hidden the gas drums! It was clear that the Viscount had talked. But Édouard could find no gas.

"How much gas did the Viscount turn over to you?" I asked Édouard.

"One thousand litres," replied Édouard.

"Why, he should have given you sixteen hundred litres. Did he keep the best gasoline for himself?"

The next day Édouard searched the Viscount's camp and found what was left of the six hundred litres. The Viscount later came over and called us blackguards.

In the Maquis there was much gallantry in the actual fighting, but when it came to getting the supplies we needed to carry out our missions we were not too scrupulous.

29 · Secret Mission

THE GASOLINE episode marked the end of our Maquis warfare. The Germans stopped coming through Châteauroux. An army of 20,000 who had recently left the city became so disgusted at being shot at that they surrendered en masse seventy miles north. Alex and I had a certificate of service printed, which we signed and distributed to our men. Then we relinquished our men to their French commanders and took a room in a hotel in Fresselines. We played two-handed poker, and made plans to tour the Riviera.

Our stay at Fresselines called for two banquets daily, at which we were the guests of honor. We were plied with the best food and the choicest wines. Dinner would begin at one in the afternoon and end at four-thirty; supper, at seven and end, maybe, at midnight. We bulged at the seams. Our brains were fogged with cognac and champagne. Alcohol and food began to fatigue us. We were forced to attend head-shaving ceremonies. The French were on a spree of shaving the heads of female collaborators, some of them pretty prostitutes whose only crime had been sleeping with Germans. When these ceremonies were over we would drink heavily to forget the sight. After the excitement of fighting our life was monotonous.

We visited Oradour-sur-Glâne, the place which the Germans had wiped out. In this once prosperous town of twelve hundred people not a house remained standing, and only half a dozen persons were alive to tell the horrible story. We talked to three who escaped. This was how it happened. The German S.S. headquarters in Limoges decided to punish the French for helping the Resistance. They chose to make an example of Oradour-sur-Glâne because they had heard that the villagers there had been sheltering Maquis soldiers. Three hundred German S.S. troops arrived early one afternoon and set up guards around the town. Those who lived within the town boundaries were to be shot. Those who lived outside the boundaries would be left alone if they did not interfere. First the Germans gathered all the families and forced them to watch their homes burning and exploding. Then they tied the men, lined them up on their knees in barns. The women and children were forced to watch. The men were shot in the groin. While the women and children screamed and the men groaned, the barns were set aflame. The women and children were then herded into the Catholic church. A baby in its mother's arms who cried too much was seized by the legs by a German who smashed its head against the wall. When all the women and children were gathered in the church, explosives and incendiaries were lighted and thrown into their midst. Some of the victims tried to climb out of the small, high windows, but they were shot down. Their work completed, the

Germans left, singing patriotic songs of the Fatherland.

Upon my return to Fresselines I found a radio message from Gerard, telling me to meet him as soon as possible in Limoges. When I met him there, he told me: "Go to Paris as soon as possible. You will be flown back to London. You are needed for another mission."

"What's the chance of taking some time off? I've never been in France before, I'd like to look around," I asked.

"You're free to do anything you wish, but if I should be asked about you I shall be compelled to say truthfully that I gave you the orders."

"How about transportation to Paris, Gerard?"

He looked at me in amazement. "Don't you have a car?"

"Why yes, I've got three cars, one bought with operational funds, two captured from the Germans."

"Well, then, pick out the best one and drive it to Paris. That's all there is to it."

I went to tell Alex. He and Édouard and the other English officers, according to information I had gleaned from Gerard, would soon be getting movement orders from the British. Alex and I regretfully gave up our plan of touring the Riviera. The gasoline we had hidden was little use to me now. Alex would inherit my share, except what I needed for the Paris trip.

I told Édouard about my orders from Gerard, but he forbade me to take any of the cars. He said they were the property of the French Government. I told him that I had bought one; he answered that all of our operational funds had been subscribed by the French. I told him that I would turn in my vehicle to French authorities in Paris; he said that the vehicles belonged to the Department of the Creuse. In desperation, I suggested that he provide me with a chauffeur who would drive me to Paris and then return with the car; he said that he needed all available chauffeurs, since there were some forty thousand Germans in a pocket near La Rochelle. If those Germans started marching, he would need every man and vehicle. I asked him what suggestions he had for my getting to Paris.

He said, "Go back to Limoges and ask Gerard for transportation."

Why he should be so rigid, I could not understand. However, I had the cars and made a bee-line for them. Édouard had beaten me to the draw! During my absence in Limoges he had taken them away, all but one. He had overlooked this last one, the poorest of the lot. Probably he didn't even know that I had it. It was the German Simca staff car, in which I had first entered Châteauroux. I quietly drove it to a garage whose owner, sworn to secrecy, put it in shape for the Paris trip.

The day before I left for Paris, Alex came with me to Châteauroux. He knew about my plan to drive off, unknown to Édouard, who was no longer my commanding officer. We inspected the car, and found it in good running order. We then went to town for a last drink together. In the cafe we met a girl, Solange, whom I had met before. Beautiful and sophisticated, she was a friend of Édouard's brother, who was also a leader in the Maquis. I admired his choice. Solange was a Parisienne but had lived near Châteauroux during the war.

A thought struck me. I leaned over the table, and said very softly, "Solange, would you like to go to Paris?"

"Indeed I would."

"Solange, I need someone to guide me to Paris. I do not know the roads. How well do you know the roads to Paris?"

"François, I have gone to Paris twenty times from Châteauroux. I know every turn in the road."

"Very well," I said, "I am leaving at eight in the morning. If you want to go, meet me outside this cafe. But tell no one, not even Édouard's brother, that you're going to Paris, or that you're going to Paris with me. Understand? I am going on a secret mission."

With Solange in the front seat and a barrel of gas where the rear seat used to be, I headed for Paris.

On the 27th of September, I flew from Paris to London, and on the 28th reported to O.S.S. headquarters.

After listening to my reports, the O.S.S. chiefs said to me: "You have done your work well in France. For your next assignment we are going to offer you a choice. Will you parachute into a German concentration camp and arm the prisoners for revolt; or would you prefer a mission to Outer Mongolia?"

But that's another story.

www.ingramcontent.com/pod-product-compliance
Lightning Source LLC
Chambersburg PA
CBHW070050080526
44586CB00013B/988